POWER ENCOUNTER

Ministering in the Power and Anointing of the Holy Spirit

Third Edition

Denzil R. Miller

Power Encounter: Ministering in the Power and Anointing of the Holy Spirit. (Third Edition) Copyright © 2013 by Denzil R. Miller. All rights reserved. No part of this book may be reproduced, stored in a retrieval system, or transmitted in any form or by any means—electronic, mechanical, photocopy, recording, or otherwise—without prior written permission of the copyright owner, except brief quotations used in connection with reviews in magazines or newspapers.

This books is a revision of the first edition published by the author in 1993. It is very similar to the book published by Africa's Hope: *Power Ministry: How to Minister in the Spirit's Power* in 2004. It is a further updating of the Revised Edition published in 2009.

All scripture quotations, unless otherwise noted, are taken from the HOLY BIBLE, NEW INTERNATIONAL VERSION, copyright 1973, 1978, 1984 by the International Bible Society. All rights reserved.

Libraries of Congress Cataloging-in-Publication Data
Miller, Denzil R., 1946–
Power Encounter: Ministering in the Power and Anointing of the Holy Spirit
Denzil R. Miller

ISBN: 978-0-9911332-3-9

1. Teaching—Pentecostal 2. Biblical teaching— 3. Biblical studies—Holy Spirit— Healing— Miracles

Printed in the United States of America
PneumaLife Publications
Springfield, MO 65803

– CONTENTS –

Preface to Revised Edition 5
Preface to Third Edition 6
Introduction 7

Part I: Understanding Power Ministry
Chapter 1:   Power Ministry Defined 11
Chapter 2:   Power Ministry Illustrated 21
Chapter 3:   Power Ministry and the Kingdom of God . 31
Chapter 4:   Power Ministry and Preaching the Gospel . 39

Part II: Preparing for a Power Ministry
Chapter 5:   Preparation for a Power Ministry 53
Chapter 6:   The Baptism in the Holy Spirit and
             Power Ministry 65
Chapter 7:   Spiritual Gifts and Power Encounter 75
Chapter 8   Pastoring the Spiritual Gifts 83
Chapter 9:   Divine Guidance and Power Encounter . . . 93
Chapter 10: The Weapons of our Warfare 103

Part III: The "How To" of a Power Ministry
Chapter 11: How to Heal the Sick 113
Chapter 12: How to Cast out Demons 125
Chapter 13: How to Pray with Believers to be Filled
             with the Spirit 135
Chapter 14: Power Ministry and Campaign Evangelism 147

Appendix 1 155
Appendix 2 161
Bibliography 165
Other Books By the Author 167

– Preface –
to the Revised Edition

This book is a revision of the book *Power Encounter: Ministering in the Power and Anointing of the Holy Spirit.* In this revision the following changes were made from the original version published in 1993:

I have sought to edit and reformat the book to make it more readable. I have also divided Chapter 6, "The Holy Spirit and Power Encounter," into two chapters: "The Baptism in the Holy Spirit and Power Encounter" and "Gifts of the Holy Spirit and Power Encounter." In the chapter on gifts of the Holy Spirit I have added a new section entitled "Releasing Spiritual Gifts." I have also added chapters on "Pastoring the Spiritual Gifts" and "Power Ministry and Campaign Evangelism." We trust that these changes will make this edition of the book even more usable than the first.

Power Encounter was originally written as a textbook for training African pastors and church leaders at the Assemblies of God School of Theology in Lilongwe, Malawi where I taught for more than a decade. It was then picked up and published in an expanded, more academic, version by Discovery Books, Springfield, Missouri, USA, under the title *Power Ministry: A Handbook for Pentecostal Preachers.* This version of the book has been translated and published into eight languages and is used as a textbook throughout Africa. Those who want to use the book in a classroom setting may want to contact Discovery Books.

This revised version of the book is rewritten with a broader readership in mind. I have removed many of the study aids in order that the text may flow without interruption. I have, nevertheless, retained the content and reflection questions and placed them at the end of each chapter.

– PREFACE –
TO THE THIRD EDITION

This book, *Power Encounter: Ministering in the Power and Anointing of the Holy Spirit: Third Edition* is an update of the "Revised Edition" published in 2009. In this newest release of the book by PnuemaLife Publishers a number of typographical errors have been corrected and select sentence have been reworded for greater clarity.

To date, the book has been translated into French, Portuguese, Kiswahili, Chichewa, Kinyarwanda, Malagasy, and Urdu. Under the title, *Power Ministry* (published by Africa's Hope, Discovery Books) it is being used throughout Africa in Bible schools and seminaries as a primary textbook to train African pastors in the theology and practice of ministry in the supernatural. It has also been used as a supplemental reader in Bible colleges and seminaries in America.

We commend this latest edition of book to you the reader and trust that it will help to encourage and equip you to preach Christ to the lost with signs following.

– INTRODUCTION –

In recent years there has been a call from church leaders and Bible school administrators for a course of study dealing with issues that daily effect the lives and ministries of Majority World pastors, evangelists, and church leaders—issues concerning the role of spiritual power in ministry. Many are asking, "How can we effectively minister in the power and anointing of the Holy Spirit?" "How can we pray for the sick, and see them healed?" "How can we lead our members into the experience of the baptism in the Holy Spirit?" This book was written to address these vital concerns.

The design of this book is threefold: First, it seeks to lay a biblical foundation for a power ministry. It is only on such a firm foundation that a credible, lasting ministry in the Spirit can be built. This issue is addressed in Part I, "Understanding Power Ministry." Next, this book deals with the personal preparation one needs to minister in the power of the Holy Spirit. What kind of person should a "power minister" be? What things should he or she know and experience before entering into such a ministry? These issues are addressed in Part II, "Preparation for a Power Ministry." Finally, I seek to offer practical advice on how one may actually *do* power ministry. This is the aim of Part III, "The 'How To' of Power Ministry."

It is my sincere desire that this book will serve as a practical, on-the-job-training manual for those who are sincerely seeking to obey the command of Jesus to preach the gospel with signs following (Mark 16:15-20).

– Part I–
Understanding Power Ministry

– Chapter 1 –

Power Ministry Defined

When Jesus returned to heaven He did not leave His church powerless. He gave to it all the power it needed to get the job done. He promised that He would give it power to evangelize the whole world (Acts 1:8). He first fulfilled that promise on the Day of Pentecost when He poured out the Holy Spirit on the waiting disciples (Acts 2:1-4). As a result, the New Testament church went out and ministered in great power and with amazing results. Some have described the method of the early church as power evangelism. In this chapter we will introduce this concept. We will do this by first discussing the need for power ministry in the church today. We will then define certain key terms that relate to the subject.

THE NEED FOR A POWER MINISTRY

As did the early church, the church today still needs power if it is to fulfill its God-given mandate of evangelizing all nations before Jesus comes again (Matt. 24:14). There are at least four reasons the church must have a ministry filled with the God's power:

We Are Involved in a War
The Bible clearly teaches that we who call ourselves the children of God are involved in a great spiritual war. We wage this war against the devil and his demonic legions. Jesus taught that our

Chapter 1: Power Ministry Defined

"enemy ... is the devil" (Matt. 13:39, cf., Luke 10:19). Paul also spoke of this spiritual conflict:

> For our struggle is not against flesh and blood, but against the rulers, against the authorities, against the powers of this dark world and against the spiritual forces of evil in the heavenly realms (Eph. 6:12).

Paul further wrote that we must use powerful spiritual weapons to successfully wage this spiritual warfare: "The weapons we fight with are not the weapons of the world. On the contrary, they have divine power to demolish strongholds" (2 Cor. 10:4). The strongholds that the apostle spoke of are spiritual strongholds set up by the enemy of our souls, the devil. In order to wage this war against the devil we must know how to minister in the power of the Spirit.

The Enemy Has Power

A second reason we need a ministry of power is that our enemy, the devil, is a powerful foe. Jesus spoke of "all the power of the enemy" (Luke 10:19). Throughout the earth Satan has mobilized a vast and dedicated army of demonic forces, committed to opposing the spread of the gospel (2 Cor. 4:4). If we are to defeat the devil, we must meet his power with even greater power. We can do this only in the power of the Holy Spirit.

The Task Is Great

Another important reason we need a power ministry is that our task is so great that a power ministry is the only way we will ever accomplish it. As mentioned above, our God-given task is to preach the gospel in all the world (Matt. 28:19-20; Mark 16:15-16). Today there remain more than 4 billion or more people who have not had an adequate witness of the gospel. How are we going to reach these masses of people, many living in lands controlled by religious systems bitterly opposed the spread of Christianity? Jesus promised us that He would give us power to accomplish this task: "But you will receive power when the Holy Spirit comes on you; and you will be my witnesses in Jerusalem, and in all Judea and Samaria, and to the ends of the earth" (Acts 1:8). He also said that, as we go to preach the gospel, He would confirm His word with powerful signs following:

> Go into all the world and preach the good news to all creation ... And these signs will accompany those who believe: In my name they will drive out demons; they will speak in new tongues; they will pick up snakes with their hands; and when they drink deadly poison, it will not hurt them at all; they will place their hands on sick people and they will get well. (Mark 16:15, 17)

What a wonderful promise! According to Jesus, the way to advance His kingdom in the world is by force, that is, in the power of the Holy Spirit. He said, "From the days of John the Baptist until now, the kingdom of heaven has been forcefully advancing, and forceful men lay hold of it" (Matt. 11:12).

Power Ministry Works

A final reason we must be involved in power ministry is because power ministry works. The tremendous success of the early church can be attributed in large part to the fact that it moved in supernatural power.

What was true for the early church is also true today. It has been pointed out that "on a worldwide scale 70% of all church growth is among Pentecostal and charismatic groups."[1] These groups are, of course, the very ones who believe in and expect the power of the Holy Spirit to be manifested their midst. John Wimber quotes C. Peter Wagner as saying, "There is a remarkably close relationship between growth of the churches today and the healing ministry ... When the gospel first penetrates a region, if we don't go with the understanding of and use of the supernatural power of the Holy Spirit, we just don't make much headway..."[2]

If we want to see New Testament results in our evangelism efforts today, we must employ New Testament methods. We must take hold of the same power that the early church had. We must

---

[1] John Wimber, *Power Evangelism*, (San Francisco: Harper and Row Publishers, 1986), 31.

[2] Ibid, 39.

learn, as they did, how to move and minister in the power of the Holy Spirit.

THE TERMS DEFINED

To have a clear understanding of what power ministry is, we need to accurately define the term. We also need to define the companion terms that have come to be associated with ministry in the supernatural.

Power Ministry
Throughout this book we will be using the term *power ministry*. Power ministry, as we will use it in this study, is any ministry in the supernatural, originating with the Spirit of God, used to advance the kingdom of God in the earth. It includes signs, wonders, healings, anointed preaching, the casting out of demons, the manifestation of spiritual gifts, or any other demonstrations of God's power and presence. Its purpose, as stated above, is to advance His kingdom in the earth.

Power Encounter
Another term used in power ministry is *power encounter,* the term found in the title of this book. We can define this term in two ways: We can define it very narrowly or we can define it more broadly. Defined narrowly, power encounter deals strictly with confronting the powers of darkness (demons) in the power of Jesus' name and in the power of the Holy Spirit. Wimber quotes Allen Tippet who defines power encounter as "the clashing of the kingdom of God with the kingdom of Satan."[3] Peter Wagner gives a similar definition: "A power encounter is a visible, practical demonstration that Jesus Christ is more powerful than the false gods or spirits worshiped or feared by a people group."[4] While we

---

[3]Ibid, (quoted from Allen Tippett, *People Movements in Southeast Polynesia).*

[4]Opal Reddin, ed., *Power Encounter, A Pentecostal Perspective* (Springfield, MO: Central Bible College, 1989), 4.

Chapter 1: Power Ministry Defined

do not disagree with these definitions, we feel they are too narrow for our present study.

Defined more broadly, a power encounter is any outward demonstration of God's sovereign power used to advance His kingdom in the earth. John Wimber stated that

> any system or force that must be overcome for the gospel to be believed is cause for a power encounter... The expulsion of demons is most dramatic, though power encounters are far from limited only to those where Satan takes the form of the demonic... When the kingdom of God comes into direct contact with the kingdom of the world (when Jesus meets Satan), there is conflict.[5]

That is, a power encounter.

Truth Encounter

A *truth encounter* is any clear declaration of the gospel of Jesus Christ either preceding or following a power encounter. While a power encounter challenges the powers of darkness, a truth encounter challenges the false teachings of a religion or society holding people in bondage. It is essential that a truth encounter always accompany a power encounter. This topic will be discussed more fully in Chapter 4.

Power Healing

For our present study we will divide divine healing into two categories. The first category we will call *covenant healing*. Covenant healing is healing as provided through Christ's atoning work on the cross (Isa. 53:4-5; cf. Matt. 8:16-17). This is the healing that He has provided for all of God's covenant people; that is, those who have made Christ their Lord and Savior. Jesus referred to this kind of healing as "the children's bread" (Matt. 15:25). Along with salvation, it is part of Christ's wonderful provision for his children that he made at the cross.

A second classification of healing is *power healing*. By power

---

[5] Wimber, 16.

healing we mean healing that is used to demonstrate the presence and power of God's kingdom. Here God often heals even nonbelievers. This kind of healing is used together with the proclamation of the gospel. It confirms the truth of what is preached. It is sometimes called "signs and wonders" in the gospels and Acts.

Power Evangelism

Power evangelism results when we combine a power encounter with a truth encounter. It is illustrated Figure 1.1.

**Power Encounter + Truth Encounter
= Power Evangelism**

Figure 1.1

According to Wimber, power evangelism "is the explanation of the gospel [that] comes with a demonstration of God's power through signs and wonders... Power evangelism is evangelism that is preceded and undergirded by supernatural demonstrations of God's presence."[6] Power evangelism takes place when there is a demonstration of God's supernatural power *plus* a clear, convincing presentation of the gospel.

Signs and Wonders

A term frequently occurring in the book of Acts is *signs and wonders.* The term first appears in Acts 2:22, where it refers to the ministry of Jesus. It is mentioned again in 2:43, immediately after the Day of Pentecost, where it describes the ministry of the church: "Everyone was filled with awe, and many wonders and miraculous signs were done by the apostles."
In Scripture the words *signs* and *wonders* are often used together, thus showing how they function hand in hand. A sign is something

---

[6]Ibid, 35.

that points to something else. In the New Testament a sign (Greek: *sēmeion*) is a miraculous happening that points to the fact that the kingdom of God has come, and that the message of the gospel is true. Jesus promised that God will confirm the preaching of the gospel with "signs following" (Mark 16:15). The same passage says that signs confirmed the message of the gospel as it was preached by the disciples (v. 20). As we go to preach the gospel, we too can expect God to confirm the message with signs following.

> **Signs and wonders in New Testament evangelism:**
> Acts 4:29-30; 5:12; 6:8; 14:3; Rom.15:19; Heb. 2:3, 4

Figure 1.2

The word *wonder* (Greek: *tera*) speaks of a miraculous work of God that causes the beholder to marvel—as when Jesus healed the demonized boy: "And they were all amazed at the greatness of God ... [and] everyone was marveling at all that Jesus did" (Luke 9:43).

In Acts the wonder of the people included utter amazement (2:7; 3:10), being filled with awe (2:43), perplexity (2:12), hearts filled with praise to God (4:21), great fear (5:5, 11), great joy (8:8), astonishment (8:13), and even saving faith (9:42, cf., 1 Cor. 2:4-5). Jesse K. Moon cites seven functions of signs and wonders in New Testament evangelism:

1. To attest to Christ's messiahship, and cause people to believe in Him (Acts 2:22; Heb.2:4).
2. To attract attention to the gospel.
3. As an evidence that Christ is the living (resurrected) Lord of the Church.
4. To verify the authenticity of the preached word (Acts 4:29, 30; 14:3; Rom.15:19; Heb.2:3-4).
5. To identify the true believers and the true religion (2 Cor. 12:12; Mark 16:15-18).
6. To meet human need.

Chapter 1: Power Ministry Defined

7. To advance the kingdom of God in the earth (Acts 5:12-14; 8:5-13).[7]

For all of the above reasons we should sincerely pray that signs and wonders will be a part of our ministry of the gospel today, just as they were in the days of the apostles.

Spirit-empowered preaching accompanied by supernatural signs and wonders is a vital key to our reaching the world with the gospel. We must therefore understand clearly what it means to minister in the power of the Holy Spirit with signs following. As we do, we will begin to see New Testaments results in our evangelistic efforts. This is the purpose of this book, that you might know these things. As you read and study the following lessons, I pray that through faith and yieldedness to the Holy Spirit, you too will begin to minister in New Testament power and with New Testaments results.

FOR REVIEW AND REFLECTION

1. Be able to quote from memory and explain the Scripture verses in Ephesians that states that we are involved in a spiritual war.
2. Why is it important that we not use "the weapons of the world" to fight spiritual battles?
3. THINK: Some act as if the devil is just as powerful as God. Is this true? Just how powerful is he?
4. Explain why the task of the church is so great that we need a power ministry to accomplish it.
5. What is meant by the phrase, "power ministry works?" Explain your answer.
6. Name four reasons a power ministry is essential today.
7. Many today are trying to reach the world in their own strength and through human methods alone. What do you think their efforts?
8. Define *power encounter* as used in this study.
9. THINK: Name several activities that can be included in a power ministry according to our definition.

---

[7]Reddin, 238.

Chapter 1: Power Ministry Defined

10. Define *truth encounter* and tell why is it essential that a truth encounter always accompany a power encounter.
11. Define and explain the term *power ministry*.
12. Distinguish between *power healing* and *covenant healing*, both in their recipients and in their purpose.
13. Define *power evangelism*.
14. THINK: Suppose an evangelist is conducting an evangelistic campaign. He has prayed for the sick and several people have been healed. He then gives an altar call for people to be saved. Can this be properly described as power evangelism? Explain your answer.
15. Define the terms *signs* and *wonders* according to their New Testament usage.
16. What are seven purposes of signs and wonders?

Chapter 1: Power Ministry Defined

– Chapter 2 –
Power Ministry
Illustrated

"Answer me, O LORD, answer me, so these people will know that you, O Lord, are God, and that you are turning their hearts back again" (1 Kings 18:37). This is Elijah's famous prayer for fire! He had challenged the prophets of Baal to a power encounter to prove that Jehovah, and not Baal, was the true and living God. God answered Elijah's prayer sending fire from heaven to consume his water-soaked sacrifice. When the people saw what was happening, they fell on their faces and cried, "The LORD—he is God! The LORD—he is God!" (v. 39). This story is a classic example of a power encounter. In Chapter 1 we defined and defended power ministry. In this chapter we will illustrate it by citing several biblical examples.

POWER ENCOUNTER ILLUSTRATED IN THE OLD TESTAMENT

In the Old Testament contains many exciting examples of power encounter. We have chosen two as illustrations:

Moses' Challenge to the "gods" of Egypt
Read the story of how Moses challenged the pagan gods of Egypt in Exodus 7-13. As you read, keep in mind that in Exodus 12:12 God told Moses that this series of confrontations between him and Pharaoh was actually encounters between God and "all the gods of Egypt." According to Paul, these gods of Egypt were, in fact, demons (1 Cor. 10:20). Don Williams writes,

Chapter 2: Power Ministry Illustrated

Exodus 5-12 recount the mighty acts of God, his signs and wonders which fall like the London Blitz.[1] Here is an authentic "power encounter," which is a visible, practical demonstration that God is more powerful than the gods of Egypt. In each of the ten plagues, God was systematically attacking one or more of the gods of Egypt.[2]

According to Fred Haltom, God sent the various plagues to confront specific Egyptian gods:

> He sent the plagues of blood, frogs, and lice as attacks on Nu, the god of the Nile River; Hekt, goddess of the land; and Geb, the earth-god. He sent the plagues of flies, disease on the beasts, and boils on man as attacks on Scarob, the insect god; Apis, the bull god; and Thoth, the god of intelligence and medical learning. He sent the hail, locusts, and darkness as attacks on Ntu, sky goddess; Anubis guardian of the fields; and Ra, the sun god. And finally the death of all the firstborn of Egypt was an attack on Pharaoh himself, the god-king.[3]

The gods of Egypt were demonic principalities and powers holding the people in spiritual bondage. The exodus of the children of Israel from Egyptian bondage was, therefore, more than just a physical deliverance for God's people. It was also a demonstration of their spiritual deliverance from the powers of darkness, and of their freedom to worship Jehovah alone.

---

[1] The London Blitz was the bombing of the city of London, England, by German bombers in World War II.

[2] Don William, *Signs, Wonders, and the Kingdom of God* (Ann Arbor, MI: Servant Publications, 1989), 82.

[3] Fred Haltom, "Old Testament Power Encounters," *Power Encounter, A Pentecostal Perspective,* 103.

Chapter 2: Power Ministry Illustrated

Elijah's Challenge to the Prophets of Baal on Mount Carmel

From 1 Kings 18:20-46, read the exciting story about the power encounter between Elijah and the demonically inspired Canaanite god, Baal. Merril C. Unger wrote about the worship of Baal: "The presence of demonic phenomena in the Old Testament, if not actual cases of possession, is strongly suggested by such instances as the orgiastic rites of the priests of Baal."[4] Remember, Elijah was not just confronting the pagan religion of Baal worship, but he was confronting the demons who where behind the religion, giving it it's power.

Note how this confrontation involved both a power encounter and a truth encounter (1 Kings 18:21). In this encounter, Jehovah is shown to be more powerful than Baal by sending down the fire from heaven to consume Elijah's sacrifice. Elijah uses this miracle as an opportunity to preach to the people and to call upon them to follow the true and living God!

These two Old Testament power encounters showed Israel, and the pagan peoples with which they came into contact, that Jehovah is the only God worthy of our service and worship.

POWER ENCOUNTER IN THE MINISTRY OF JESUS

Jesus' ministry was full of power encounters. Through these demonstrations of power Jesus showed that He truly was the "Anointed One," sent from God. He also showed that the kingdom of God had come to overthrow the kingdom of Satan (Luke 11:20). Power encounter is illustrated in four ways in the ministry of Jesus, as follows:

In the Purpose of His Ministry

The Bible says that one of the purposes of Jesus' coming was "to destroy the devil's work" (1 John 3:8). Even the demons understood that He had come to destroy them: "Just then a man in their synagogue who was possessed by an evil spirit cried out, 'What do you want with us, Jesus of Nazareth? Have you come to

---

[4]Merril C. Unger, *Biblical Demonology* (Wheaton, IL: Scripture Press, 1971).

destroy us?'" (Mark 1:23-24).

In Luke 4:18-19 Jesus revealed His agenda for ministry. He would focus on six things:

1. *Anointing:* He would minister under the anointing of the Spirit. ("The Spirit of the Lord is upon me, because He has anointed me...")
2. *Preaching:* He would preach the gospel. ("...to preach good news to the poor.")
3. *Setting the prisoners free:* He would liberate those bound by sin and the devil. ("He has sent me to proclaim freedom to the prisoners...")
4. *Healing:* He would heal the sick. ("...and recovery of sight for the blind...")
5. *Releasing the oppressed:* He would liberate those in bondage—spiritually, physically, emotionally, religiously, and socially. ("...to release the oppressed...")
6. *Proclaiming the coming of the kingdom of God:* He would announce that the time had arrived for the coming of God's kingdom. ("...to proclaim the year of the Lord's favor.")

In the Performance of His Ministry

Not only did Jesus announce that He had come to challenge and destroy the works of the devil, He also demonstrated that fact in the actual performance of His ministry. The twofold emphasis of Jesus' ministry was preaching (and teaching) and healing (Matt. 4:23; 9:35). He often combined the two. He thus included both power encounter and truth encounter in His strategy of ministry.

There are, of course, many examples of power encounter in the ministry of Jesus. We have chosen four representative examples for our study:

1. His Wilderness Temptation (Luke 4:1-13). In His wilderness temptation Jesus came into direct conflict with Satan. Luke says that He entered into this contest being "full of the Holy Spirit" (v. 1). This was Jesus' first major power confrontation with the power of darkness. Here, at the very beginning of His ministry, Jesus demonstrated His power over, not just the demons, but over Satan himself, the prince of demons. News of their captain's defeat must

Chapter 2: Power Ministry Illustrated

have spread quickly through the demonic realm, because from this time on the demons seem to know and fear the power of Jesus (i.e., Mark 1:23-24).

2. His First Miracle in Mark (1:21-27; 34, 39; 3:10-11). Jesus' first miracle in the gospel of Mark is a typical example of Jesus' many power encounters with demons. Something about the presence of Jesus seemed to set the demons on edge. Intimidated by His very presence, they cried out in fear. Jesus commanded them to "Be quiet!" and "Come out!" They had no choice but to obey Him!

3. His Encounter with the Gadarene Demoniac (Mark 5:1-20). The story of Jesus delivering the Gadarene demoniac is the most complete example of His confronting and expelling demons recorded in Scripture. Again, as in our last example, these demons are intimidated by Jesus' presence. And again, the man is totally delivered from demons at the command of Jesus.

4. His Healing of a Demonized Boy (Mark 9:14-32). The demonized boy of Mark 9 again demonstrates how Jesus openly confronted and defeated demonic powers. As before, the demons had to obey Jesus' command. When the disciples asked why they could not cast out the demon, Jesus pointed to their lack of prayer (and fasting [NKJV]) as the cause of their powerlessness (v. 29).

Jesus, of course, did many other signs, wonders, and miracles throughout His ministry. Space does not allow us to look at all of them, however, we should make the ministry of Jesus our lifelong study. And we should seek to imitate Him in all that He said and did. We can learn much about how to heal the sick and deal with demons through a thorough study of these and the many other power encounters of Jesus.

In the Teachings of His Disciples

Not only did Jesus come to destroy the works of the devil Himself, He taught His disciples to do the same. Certainly, one reason the Bible gives to us so many details about how Jesus healed the sick, and how He delivered those in bondage, is so that we, like the twelve disciples, may be able to observe how He ministered. And then, like them, we can pattern our ministries after His.

Jesus often taught His disciples how to minister in the power of the Spirit. Twice He sent them out on training missions (Luke 9:1-6; 10:1-23). On the second occasion Jesus had the seventy-two report back to Him (10:17). After receiving their report, He took time to instruct them. He told them that He has given to them authority over "all the power of the enemy" (Luke 10:19).

In the very next chapter Jesus gave His disciples an extended teaching on how to deal with demonic powers (Luke 11:14-26). You may now want to carefully read and study this important passage.

In the Passing on of His Ministry

In the passing on of His ministry to His disciples, Jesus made it clear that they too would be involved in power ministry. When Jesus appointed the twelve apostles, He sent them out "to preach and to have authority to drive out demons" (Mark 3:14). They were to have the same twofold ministry He had had—involving both power encounter and truth encounter.

In Luke 9 Jesus sent out the Twelve. Before doing this, however, He gave to them power and authority to drive out demons and to cure diseases. He then sent them out to preach the kingdom of God and to heal the sick (vv. 1-2). Again, the twofold ministry of demonstration and declaration (power and preaching) is emphasized.

In Mark's version of the Great Commission, Jesus, after commanding His disciples to preach the gospel in all the world, promised them that they could expect the same signs to follow their ministries as followed His (16:15-18). Then, according to verses 19 and 20, His disciples went out and fulfilled the twofold ministry of power and preaching. We, like those who first heard those words, must also go in the power of the Holy Spirit, preaching the gospel with signs following.

Jesus' final and most dramatic act of passing on His ministry of power to his followers took place on the Day of Pentecost. On that day He gave to them the same power that had enabled Him in His ministry (Acts 10:38). This happened when "they were all filled with the Holy Spirit and began to speak with other tongues as the Spirit enabled them" (Acts 2:4). This same Pentecostal power is available to us today so that we too might do the works of Jesus (John 14:26, cf., 16:7).

Chapter 2: Power Ministry Illustrated

POWER ENCOUNTER IN THE MINISTRY OF THE EARLY CHURCH

Having received the power of the Spirit on the day of Pentecost, the early disciples went out and ministered as Jesus had taught them. As was His, their ministries were characterized by both declaration and demonstration. They not only talked about the gospel, they demonstrated that the kingdom of God had indeed come in great power.

Observations About the Ministry of the Early Church

The ministry of the church in the book of Acts is a continuation of the ministry of Jesus who was anointed and empowered by the Holy Spirit to do His mighty works. The book of Acts begins with these words: "In my former book, O Theophilus, I wrote about all that Jesus began to do and to teach" (Acts 1:1). Note the phrase *began to do and teach.* The implication is clear: Now that Jesus had returned to heaven, the church would continue His ministry, including both His powerful words and works. And this is just what the early church did.

Signs and wonders were central to the ministry of the early church. A careful reading of Acts reveals that, in performing their ministries, the apostles closely followed the twofold pattern established by Jesus of demonstration and declaration. In addition to powerful proclamation of the gospel, their ministry included signs and wonders, healings, praying with believers to receive the Holy Spirit, the expelling of demons, miracles with nature and food, the resuscitation of the dead, tongues, prophecy, visions, and other extraordinary miracles.

Often, as a result of a demonstration of God's power, amazement and wonder came upon the people. The gospel was then preached with great persuasive power, and hundreds were saved. The same can happen today, if we, like the early church, will follow the twofold pattern set by Jesus.

Examples of Power Encounter in the Early Church

In the following exercise you will be able to examine two examples of power ministry in Acts for yourself:

Chapter 2: Power Ministry Illustrated

The Day of Pentecost. Carefully read Acts 2:1-41 and answer the following questions:

1. What demonstrations of God's power took place on the Day of Pentecost?
2. What was the reaction of the crowd to those demonstrations of power?
3. Does a truth encounter also occur? If so, describe it.
4. What were the results of this power encounter?

Healing at the Beautiful Gate. Carefully read Acts 3:1-26. Answer the same four questions as you did in the previous example:

1. What demonstration of God's power took place at the Beautiful Gate?
2. What was the reaction of the crowd to this demonstration of power?
3. Does a truth encounter also occur? If so, describe it.
4. What were the results of this power encounter?

What conclusions can we draw from this study?

FOR REFLECTION AND REVIEW

1. Why do we say that the ten plagues sent by God upon Egypt are examples of power encounters?
2. Why do we say that Elijah's contest against the prophets of Baal is both a power encounter and a truth encounter?
3. What two things did Jesus show through His power encounters?
4. What does the Bible say was a primary purpose of Jesus' ministry on earth?
5. THINK: What are some of the works of the devil that Jesus came to destroy?
6. What was the six-fold agenda of Jesus' ministry according to Luke 4:18-19?
7. What was the twofold emphasis of Jesus' ministry?
8. How did Jesus demonstrate His power over Satan in His first encounter with him?
9. Why did the demons cry out when the saw Jesus?

Chapter 2: Power Ministry Illustrated

10. What methods did Jesus use in delivering the Gadarene demoniac in Mark 5:8?
11. THINK: What were the demons doing to harm the demonized boy of Mark 9? How did Jesus set him free? Why were the disciples unable to cast the demons out?
12. List three occasions when Jesus sought to teach His disciples how to have a power ministry.
13. What ways did Jesus use to pass on His ministry of power to His disciples? Which was the most lasting and dramatic?
14. Describe the ministry of the early church as to how it related to the ministry of Jesus.
15. Make a list of the kinds of miracles that followed the ministries of the apostles?

– Chapter 3 –
Power Encounter
and the
Kingdom of God

What do you think of when you hear the term *the kingdom of God?* Most Christians have no clear understanding of subject. This is tragic, since the kingdom of God is one of the most important themes of the New Testament. An accurate understanding of the kingdom of God is essential to power ministry.[1] This chapter will address this important subject. It will discuss three issues concerning the kingdom of God: First, it will define the kingdom; then, it will discuss how the kingdom of God must come into the world in power; and finally, it will talk about the proclamation of the kingdom.

THE KINGDOM OF GOD DEFINED

When we think the word *kingdom* in this context, we should not think of a place or a geographical region, but of the rule or a reign of a king. The kingdom of God is, then, the rule or reign of God. It speaks of God's sovereign authority over His creation. So, when we say that the kingdom of God has come, we mean that God has come to set up His reign and rule.

Two Tenses of the Kingdom

---

[1] A detailed exposition of the kingdom of God can be found in the author's book, *The Kingdom and the Power: The Kingdom of God: A Pentecostal Interpretation.*

Chapter 3: Power Ministry and the Kingdom of God

The kingdom of God may be thought of as having both a present and a future tense. The kingdom has come, but it is also coming. "We can sum up the thought this way:" writes Don Williams, "the kingdom is really here, but not fully here. Believers, then, live in a kingdom come and coming."[2] Let's look more closely at these two tenses of the kingdom:

The kingdom of God is already present. It came in the person and through the work of Jesus Christ (Luke 17:20-21). Later, it came again on the Day of Pentecost (Mark 9:1; Acts 1:8). It was by pouring out the Spirit at Pentecost that Jesus transferred His kingdom ministry and power to His church. According to Peter Kuzmic, "Men are now seizing [the kingdom of God] or being violently seized by it (Matt. 11:12, 13; Luke 16:16). The overthrow of Satan's reign has already begun, the power of the future age is already operative in the present world, and the messianic blessings are available to those who respond."[3]

The kingdom of God is coming. The kingdom of God will come in fullness at the second coming of Christ (Rev. 11:15). So, while the kingdom of God has already come, and the invasion of the kingdom of Satan has begun, there remains a future establishing of God's kingdom rule on the earth. This will happen when the Son of Man shall come "in power and great glory" (Matt. 24:30), defeat the devil, and set up His righteous reign on earth.

This profound truth (i.e., the truth that the kingdom has come, and is yet coming) explains much of our present experience. It explains our triumph over Satan on one hand, and our continuing warfare with him on the other. It explains why many today are dramatically healed, and yet many remain sick and die. It explains why we have power over demons, and yet Satan continues to exercise control over many people and many areas of our world. The kingdom of God has come in part; however, someday it will come in completeness. Now we have power and authority over

---

[2] Williams, 107.

[3] Peter Kuzmic, "Kingdom of God," *Dictionary of Pentecostal and Charismatic Movements*, (Grand Rapids: Zondervan Publishing House, 1988), 523.

Chapter 3: Power Ministry and the Kingdom of God

demons, but then all the powers of darkness will be completely and finally defeated.

THE COMING OF THE KINGDOM OF GOD

Jesus came to announce the reign of God. The message of the kingdom of God was the central theme of His preaching. Listen to His words:

> I must preach the good news of the kingdom of God to the other towns also, because that is why I was sent. (Luke 4:43, see also Matt. 4:23; Mark 1:14-15; Luke 8:1, 9:11)

According to Kuzmic, "The idea of the kingdom of God occupies a place of supreme importance in the teaching and mission of Jesus. This 'master-thought' of Jesus, as it has been called, is the central theme of his proclamation and the key to understanding his ministry."[4]

Jesus began His ministry by announcing, "The time has come ... the kingdom of God is near" (Mark 1:15, cf. Matt. 3:1). In beginning His ministry this way, Jesus was announcing the coming of God's rule to this earth. He was saying that the kingdom of God had arrived, and was now within reach of anyone who will take hold of it. The "year of the Lord's favor" (Luke 4:19) had come. God had come in the person of Jesus Christ to take back what was His, and to bring the blessings of heaven to an earth-bound humanity.

The kingdom of God was also the central theme of the preaching of Christ's disciples. Whenever Jesus sent them out to minister, He instructed them to proclaim the kingdom of God and to demonstrate its power (Matt. 10:7; Luke 9:2; 10:9, 11).

The Coming of God's Kingdom Results in Conflict

The kingdom of God came first in Christ. It now comes in His church, empowered by the Holy Spirit. The kingdom is forcefully advancing to repossess what is rightfully God's. Now, because

---

[4] Kuzmic, 522.

God's kingdom has come, confrontation has resulted. Satan, the usurper, is vigorously opposing God, and, therefore, a violent spiritual war has broken out (Eph. 6:12).

The Coming of God's Kingdom is with Power

When God's kingdom comes, it does not come timidly, nor does it come apologetically—it comes in dynamic power. Paul said, "For the kingdom of God is not a matter of talk but of power" (1 Cor. 4:20). In fact, the kingdom of God can come no other way. Because of Satan's stubborn resistance to the coming of the kingdom, it must advance in power. The supplanter must be evicted by force. Jesus said,

> But if I drive out demons by the Spirit of God, then the kingdom of God has come upon you. Or again, how can anyone enter a strong man's house and carry off his possessions unless he first ties up the strong man? Then he can rob his house. (Matt. 12:28-29)

Thus, the church must move in the power of God's Spirit if it is to effectively advance His kingdom in this world. On one occasion Jesus told of a day when His disciples would see the kingdom of God come in power: "I tell you the truth, some who are standing here will not taste death before they see the kingdom of God come with power" (Mark 9:1).

The disciples, of course, had seen the power of God's kingdom manifested in the ministry of Jesus. However, when Jesus made this statement, He was referring to an event that would take place in the relatively near future. It would occur prior to the death of some of those present. Jesus was speaking of the Day of Pentecost, when His church would be clothed with power from on high (Luke 24:49). Today, the kingdom of God comes in power each time someone is filled or otherwise touched by the Spirit of God (Acts 1:8).

Signs of the Coming Kingdom

Signs, wonders, and miracles show that the kingdom of God is present. They are a foreshadowing of what will be once the

Chapter 3: Power Ministry and the Kingdom of God

kingdom of God has come in fullness. Healing today is a foreshadowing of the ending of all suffering and sickness (Rev. 21:4). The casting out of demons signals God's invasion of the realm of Satan, and foreshadows Satan's final destruction when Jesus returns (Rev. 20:10).

Jesus taught us to pray, "Your kingdom come" (Matt. 6:10). In doing this He was instructing us to pray for at least three things:

1. We are to pray for people to be saved. The kingdom of God comes personally to a individual when he or she is born again. This could have been what Jesus meant when He said, "... the kingdom of God is within you" (Luke 17:21).

2. We are to pray for people to be filled with the Spirit, healed, and delivered from demonic affliction. The kingdom of God comes in power when people are thus empowered by the Spirit or set free by the power of God (Matt. 12:28 and Luke 11:20, cf. 10:9).

3. We are to pray that Jesus will come again (Rev. 22:20). When Jesus comes again He will defeat Satan and establish His sovereign reign in the earth. Then the kingdom of God will have come in its fullness.

THE PREACHING OF THE KINGDOM OF GOD

Jesus sent out His disciples to preach the gospel of the kingdom. They were to announce that God, through Christ, had come to set up His reign on earth. We too have been called to proclaim the same message. Jesus said, "And this gospel of the kingdom will be preached in the whole world as a testimony to all nations, and then the end will come" (Matt. 24:14).

In the four gospels Jesus spoke of the kingdom of God, or its equivalent, the kingdom of heaven, over 90 times. When Jesus commissioned and sent out the Twelve, he gave them special instructions:

> When Jesus had called the Twelve together, he gave them power and authority to drive out all demons and to cure diseases, and he sent them out to preach the kingdom of God and to heal the sick. (Luke 9:1-2)

As you go, preach this message: "The kingdom of heaven is near.

Chapter 3: Power Ministry and the Kingdom of God

Heal the sick, raise the dead, cleanse those who have leprosy, drive out demons. Freely you have received, freely give." (Matt. 10:7-8)

He gave a similar mandate to the Seventy-two: "Heal the sick who are there and tell them, 'The kingdom of God is near you'" (Luke 10:9).

During the forty days after His resurrection, Jesus often "spoke about the kingdom of God" (Acts 1:3). What were the kingdom topics about which He spoke? One very important topic was the importance of being filled with the Spirit (Acts 1:4-5). He also spoke of witnessing in the power of the Spirit (Acts 1:8). The preaching of the kingdom of God continued throughout the book of Acts. When Philip went down to Samaria he proclaimed Christ (8:5), worked miracles (8:6), and "preached the good news of the kingdom of God and the name of Jesus Christ" (8:12). In Ephesus Paul taught for three months concerning the kingdom of God (19:8; 20:25). Later, in Rome, he "preached the kingdom of God and taught about the Lord Jesus Christ" (28:30).

The Gospel of the Kingdom Defined

What then is the gospel of the kingdom which Jesus commissioned the church to proclaim? Several definitions of the term have been offered. Some ultra-dispensationalists teach that the gospel of the kingdom is not the gospel that we preach today, but it is simply the announcement of the coming of Christ that will only be preached during the tribulation period after the church has been raptured. This could not be true since Jesus has commanded us to preach the gospel of the kingdom prior to His coming again (Matt. 24:14; Acts 1:8).

George Eldon Ladd defines the gospel of the kingdom as "the Good News about the Kingdom of God." He further states, "The gospel of the Kingdom is the Gospel which was proclaimed by the apostles in the early church."[5] While not disagreeing with Ladd, we

---

[5]George Eldon Ladd, "The Gospel of the Kingdom," *Perspectives on the World Christian Movement, A Reader* (Pasadena, CA: William Carey Library, 1981), 59.

Chapter 3: Power Ministry and the Kingdom of God

would like to add to his definition: The gospel of the kingdom is, indeed, the good news of the kingdom of God. It is, further, the good news that the King has come, and that He has defeated His enemies and the enemies of mankind at the cross and through His glorious resurrection from the dead. It is, further, the good news announced using the same methods as did Jesus and the apostles. Tom Marshall gives this powerful insight into the gospel of the kingdom: "The Gospel of the Kingdom," he writes, "is the Gospel of salvation with the addition of the powers of the age to come."[6]

Jesus and the early church not only announced the coming of God's kingdom, and the overthrow of Satan's kingdom, they also demonstrated the powers of the world to come by healing the sick, driving out demons, and other demonstrations of the Spirit's power. Jesus spoke about how the kingdom of God forcefully advances:

> From the days of John the Baptist until now, the kingdom of heaven has been forcefully advancing, and forceful men lay hold of it. (Matt. 11:12)

> The Law and the Prophets were proclaimed until John. Since that time, the good news of the kingdom of God is being preached, and everyone is forcing his way into it. (Luke 16:16)

We are not only to be proclaimers of Jesus' message, but we are to be imitators of His methods—and demonstrators of His kingdom's power. Don Williams wrote, "If we adopt Jesus' agenda for ministry, we will pray down the anointing power of God, and with his Spirit upon us, evangelize the poor, bring release to the captives, recovery of sight to the blind, liberate the oppressed, and announce to the world, 'this is the favorable year of the Lord' (Luke 4:18-19)."[7]

When Jesus commissioned the Twelve, He "gave them power and authority to drive out all demons and to cure diseases, and he

---

[6]Tom Marshall, *Foundations for a Healing Ministry*, (West Sussex, ENG: Sovereign World, 1988), 51.

[7]Williams, 139.

sent them out to preach the kingdom of God and to heal the sick" (Luke 9:1). Later, when He sent out the Seventy-two, He told them, "When you enter a town and are welcomed, eat what is set before you. Heal the sick who are there and tell them, 'The kingdom of God is near you'" (Luke 10:8-9). That's what it means to preach the gospel of he kingdom. It means to preach the gospel, but it means to do it in the power of the Holy Spirit with signs following. We have been called by God and anointed by His Spirit to do just that.

FOR REFLECTION AND REVIEW

1. Define the kingdom of God.
2. What is meant by the phrase "the kingdom of God has two tenses"? What does this truth mean to us today?
3. How does the two tenses of the kingdom of God explain much of our present experience?
4. What did Jesus mean when He said, "The kingdom of God is near?"
5. Why does the coming of the kingdom of God result in conflict?
6. When can we say the kingdom of God has come in power?
7. How do the signs of the kingdom that we see today relate to the future coming of the kingdom of God in fullness?
8. When Jesus told us to pray, "Your kingdom come," what three things was He telling us to pray for?
9. Cite five scripture texts that speak of preaching the gospel of the kingdom.
10. As we go preaching the gospel of the kingdom, how should we do it, and what should accompany our preaching?

– Chapter 4 –

Power Encounter and Preaching the Gospel

Power encounter is an essential part of true gospel preaching. In the last chapter we talked about preaching the gospel of the kingdom. In this chapter we will expand on the subject of preaching of the gospel and how it relates to power ministry. A thoughtful study of the ministries of Jesus and the early disciples reveals that power encounter was an essential part of both. Power encounters often accompanied—and usually preceded—the declaration of the gospel message. A powerful witness to the truth of their message resulted, with many people being saved.

TWO ESSENTIAL ELEMENTS OF AUTHENTIC GOSPEL WITNESS

The power of the gospel must be demonstrated and it's truth must be proclaimed. The two essential elements of authentic gospel witness are demonstration and proclamation. By proclamation we mean the preaching of the gospel. By demonstration we mean the signs, wonders, and miracles that accompany the preaching of the gospel. This is "show and tell" at its very best. The powers of darkness must be defeated, and then the victory can be proclaimed.

Getting First Things First

Jesus taught us that we must often do spiritual battle before the gospel can be effectively proclaimed:

> But if I drive out demons by the Spirit of God, then the kingdom of God has come upon you. Or again, how can anyone enter a strong man's house and carry off his possessions unless he first ties up the strong man? *Then* he can rob his house. (Matt. 12:28-20, emphasis added)

Jesus is teaching that it is often important that we get first things first in gospel ministry. Many times we must first "tie up the strong man," *then* we can "rob his house." The strong man in the above verse can refer to Jesus and His defeat of Satan. It can further refer to a powerful demon who controls either the life of an individual, a society, or a geographical territory. His house is the place where he has set up his stronghold. His possessions represent the soul of the individual, or the souls of the people in the society he holds in bondage (see Fig 4.1).

	The Strong Man of Matthew 12:28, 29	
	When Possessing and Individual	**When Controlling a Society or Geographical Territory**
The Strong Man	A powerful demon controlling a person	A powerful demon controlling a society
The Strong Man's House	The person under the demon's control	The society under the demon's control
The Strong Man's Possessions	The person's eternal soul	The eternal souls of those people in a society

Figure 4.1

Chapter 4: Power Ministry and Preaching the Gospel

Often, before we can rob the strongman's house and carry off his possessions—that is, before we can take from him the souls of men and women he holds captive—we must first attack and overpower him.

It is significant, I believe, that the first sign that Jesus promises to those fulfilling his Great Commission is "they will drive out demons" (Mark 16:17). Many times our first order of business is to overpower the demonic forces, and then we can proclaim liberty and salvation to those he held hostage.

Power *PLUS!*

As we have already noted in Chapter 1, Christ has given to us all the tools we need to get the job done. Two powerful tools He has given us are the Holy Spirit and the gospel. The unfailing formula for a powerful and convincing gospel witness is illustrated in Figure 4.2.

The Power of the Holy Spirit +	**The Power of the Gospel** =	**Amazing Results**

Figure 4.2

Let's briefly examine each element of this formula.

The power of the Holy Spirit. Christ has given to us the power of the Holy Spirit. In Acts 1:8 Jesus promised that we will receive power when the Holy Spirit comes upon us. It is therefore essential that everyone who is involved in sharing the gospel be filled with the Holy Spirit.[1] Not only must we be filled with the Spirit, but we must also understand how to release the power of the Holy Spirit in ministry.

---

[1] See Chapter 6, "The Baptism in the Holy Spirit and Power Encounter" for a fuller treatment of this subject.

Plus the power of the gospel. Christ has also given to us the power of the gospel. It is essential that we understand this awesome power. Because of Paul's complete confidence in the gospel, he exulted, "That is why I am so eager to preach the gospel… I am not ashamed of the gospel, because it is the power of God for salvation for everyone who believes" (Rom. 1:15-16).

Note how Paul described the gospel as "the power of God for salvation." He said that the gospel has within itself the power to create faith in the lives of those who hear it: "Consequently faith comes from hearing the message, and the message is heard through the word of Christ" (Rom. 10:17). The context of this statement indicates that Paul is talking specifically about the gospel. He is saying that the gospel, the message of Christ, has an incredible power to produce faith in the hearts of those who hear it!

Jesus taught about this faith-producing power of the gospel in His Parable of the Growing Seed (Mark 4:26-29). In this parable He compared the gospel with a seed. Like a seed, the gospel contains within itself miraculous reproductive power:

> He also said, "This is what the kingdom of God is like. A man scatters seed on the ground. Night and day, whether he sleeps or gets up, the seed sprouts and grows, though he does not know how." (vv. 26-27)

How powerful is the gospel of Jesus Christ. If we will only proclaim it, it has power within itself to produce a harvest!

What then is the preaching of the gospel? It is preaching "the word of Christ" (Rom. 10:17), that is, the message of Jesus and all that He has done, all that He is doing, and all that He will do in the future. At the heart of the gospel message is the death, burial and resurrection of Christ (1 Cor. 15:1-4). We must never fail to preach this powerful message. Far too many so called "gospel preachers" seldom preach about Jesus. Let us not fail to boldly proclaim the good news of Jesus, for it alone contains the power of God to lead men to salvation (1 Cor. 1:18).

Equals amazing results. If we will faithfully combine these two elements—the power of the Holy Spirit and the power of the gospel—we can expect amazing results. This is exactly what happened in the early church in the book of Acts.

Figure 4.3
Church Growth in the Book of Acts

1:15:	"the believers . . . numbering about a hundred and twenty"
2:41:	"about three thousand were added to their number that day"
2:47:	"the Lord added to their number daily those who were being saved"
4:4:	"many who heard the message believed, and the number of men grew to about five thousand"
5:14:	"more and more men and women believed in the Lord and were added to their number"
6:1:	"In those days when the number of disciples was increasing"
6:7:	"The number of disciples in Jerusalem increased rapidly, and a large number of priests became obedient to the faith."
9:35:	"All those who lived in Lydda and Sharon ... turned to the Lord."
9:42:	"many people believed in the Lord"
11:21:	"a great number of people believed and turned to the Lord"
11:24:	"a great number of people were brought to the Lord"
13:49:	"The word of the Lord spread through the whole region"
14:1:	" a great number of Jews and Gentiles believed"
14:21:	"they . . . won a large number of disciples"
16:5:	"the churches were strengthened in the faith and grew daily in numbers"
17:4:	"Some of the Jews were persuaded and joined Paul and Silas, as did a large number of God-fearing Greeks and not a few prominent women"
19:18	"Many of those who believed now came and openly confessed their evil deeds.
19:20:	"the word of the Lord spread widely and grew in power"
19:26:	"large numbers of people here in Ephesus and in practically the whole province of Asia"

Chapter 4: Power Ministry and Preaching the Gospel

We can trace the amazing growth of the New Testament church through reading a series of verses in the book of Acts (see Fig. 4.3 below). Note how the church grew from 120 believers to many thousands in a very short time. This amazing growth was produced by combining the power of the Holy Spirit with the faithful preaching of the gospel.

POWER ENCOUNTER IN THE PREACHING AND TEACHING OF JESUS AND THE EARLY CHURCH

Both Jesus and the early church preached the gospel in the power of the Holy Spirit with signs following. Let's look briefly at each:

The Preaching and Teaching of Jesus

In His own ministry Jesus combined the teaching and preaching of the gospel with a demonstration of the power of the Holy Spirit (i.e., Matt. 4:23; 9:35). This resulted in large crowds coming to hear His message and following Him (Mark 4:24-25; 9:36).

In commissioning (Mark 3:13-15) and later sending out the Twelve (Luke 9:1-2), and the Seventy-two (10:1-16), Jesus enabled them and instructed them to drive out demons, heal the sick, and preach the gospel of the kingdom (v. 9). Finally, in giving His commission to preach the gospel in all of the world, Jesus promised power that would come only through the infilling of the Holy Spirit (Mark 15:17-18; Luke 24:48-49; John 20:21-22; Acts 1:8).

The Preaching and Teaching of the Early Church

In the Acts of the Apostles

Throughout Acts there is a clear pattern of witness. The early church consistently joined the preaching of the gospel with a demonstration of the power of the Holy Spirit. This pattern follows uniformly throughout Acts. Because of space, however, we will cite only four representatives examples:

1. The Day of Pentecost (Acts 2:1-41). The Day of Pentecost

Chapter 4: Power Ministry and Preaching the Gospel

begins with a demonstration of the power of God. The thousands of worshipers who entered the Temple courts that day had no thought, and even less desire, to listen to the preaching of Peter. Then suddenly they heard from heaven "a sound like the blowing of a violent wind" (v. 2).[2] To their amazement, they saw "what seemed to be tongues of fire that separated and came to rest on each of them" (v. 3). Then, they heard the 120 begin "to speak with other tongues as the Spirit enabled them" (v. 4).

A great "faith shift" took place in the hearts of those who were witnessing these wonderful exhibitions of God's power and presence. Instantly, because of the miracles they witnessed, their whole attitude changed. They were no longer disinterested passers by; they were now participants in the event, ready to believe and receive the gospel. When Peter stood to preach, they were vitally interested in what he had to say. And, when Peter completed his sermon, 3000 readily responded.

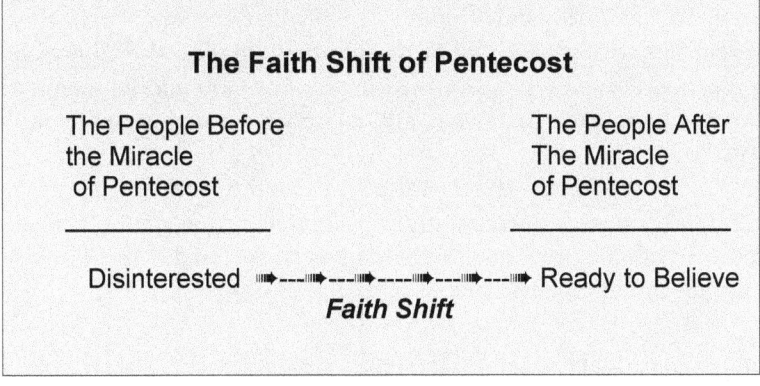

2. *The Beautiful Gate* (Acts 3:1–4:4). Our second example takes place a short time later. Again, the disciples follow the same basic pattern of combining a demonstration of the power of God

---

[2] The traditional view is that the Holy Spirit was poured out in the upper room (Acts 1:13). The author believes that it is more likely that the Spirit was poured out in the temple court (Luke 24:53).

Chapter 4: Power Ministry and Preaching the Gospel

with a clear presentation of the gospel of Christ. This event takes place at the entrance of the temple, called the Beautiful Gate. As the result of another power demonstration—the healing of a man crippled from birth—the previously disinterested crowd had a faith shift. They were "filled with wonder and amazement ... [and] were astonished and came running to them" (3:10, 11). Again, Peter stood and delivered a Christ-centered message resulting in many believing: "And the number of men grew to about five thousand" (4:4).

3. Philip in Samaria (Acts 8:1-7). We see this same pattern—the joining of a demonstration of the power of the Holy Spirit with the preaching of the gospel—continued in the ministry of Philip. The Bible says that "Philip went down to the city of Samaria and preached Christ there" (v. 5). Along with preaching the gospel, he also demonstrated God's power for "the crowds heard Philip and saw the miraculous signs he did" (v. 5). These miraculous signs included the expulsion of demons and the healing of many paralytics and cripples. As a result, the people "paid close attention" to what he said (v.6), and they "believed Philip as he preached the good news of the kingdom of God and the name of Jesus Christ" (v. 12). As a result "there was great joy in the city" (v. 8).

4. Paul in Lystra (Acts 4:8-10). A final example of the early church's practice of combining a demonstration of the Spirit's power with the proclamation of the gospel is found in the ministry of Paul in the Galatian city of Lystra:

> In Lystra there sat a man crippled in his feet, who was lame from birth and had never walked. He listened to Paul as he was speaking. Paul looked directly at him, saw that he had faith to be healed and called out, 'Stand up on your feet!' At that, the man jumped up and began to walk. (vv. 8-10)

Paul, as was his custom, used this incident as an opportunity to declare the message of Christ (vv. 7, 15-17).

If we are to see the same dramatic results today as did these New Testament evangelists, we must use the above examples as an inspiration and as a pattern for our own evangelistic endeavors.

Chapter 4: Power Ministry and Preaching the Gospel

In the Teachings of Paul

Not only is the pattern of demonstration plus proclamation illustrated in the ministries of Jesus and the early disciples, it is also clearly taught in the letters of Paul. We cite five examples:

1. *1 Corinthians 2:2-5.* In this passage Paul reviews his ministry in Corinth. He reminds the Corinthians of his method of preaching the gospel to them:

> For I resolved to know nothing while I was with you except Jesus Christ and him crucified… My message and my preaching were not with wise and persuasive words, but with a demonstration of the Spirit's power, so that your faith might not rest on man's wisdom, but on God's power.

While Paul was with the Corinthians, his ministry centered on two things: the message of "Jesus Christ and him crucified," and the "demonstration of the Spirit's power."

2. *1 Corinthians 14:23-26.* Here Paul instructed the church to expect demonstrations of the Spirit's power and presence when they gathered for worship.

3. *2 Corinthians 12:12.* In this passage Paul reminded the Corinthian believers that, while he was with them, "the things that mark an apostle—signs, wonders and miracles—were done among [you]…"

4. *Romans 15:18-20.* Paul told the Roman believers that his apostolic ministry was characterized by demonstrations of the Spirit's power:

> I will not venture to speak of anything except what Christ has accomplished through me in leading the Gentiles to obey God by *what I have said and done*—by the power of signs and miracles, through the power of the Spirit. So from Jerusalem all the way around to Illyricum, I have fully proclaimed the gospel of Christ. (emphasis added)

Note how Paul's message consisted of both what he *said* and *did*. He performed "signs and miracles, through the power of the Spirit," and he "fully proclaimed the gospel of Christ."

5. *1 Thessalonians 1:5.* Finally, Paul reminded the Thessalonians of how his gospel came to them: "Our gospel came to you

Chapter 4: Power Ministry and Preaching the Gospel

not simply with words, but also with power, with the Holy Spirit, and with deep conviction." Once again the New Testament pattern of proclamation of the gospel plus a demonstration of the power of the Spirit is evident.

In this chapter we have shown that there are two important elements in a true witness of the gospel of Christ. One is a demonstration of the power of God, the other is a clear presentation of the gospel. If our witness is to be as effective as that of Jesus and the apostles, we too must learn to use both of these methods.

FOR REFLECTION AND REVIEW

1. What are the two essential elements of authentic gospel witness?
2. What must we often do before we can preach the gospel with effectiveness in certain areas?
3. Using the chart entitled, "The Strong Man of Matthew 12:28-29," answer the following questions:
    - Who is the strong man when possessing an individual?
    - Who is the strong man when controlling a society?
    - What is the strong man's house when possessing an individual?
    - What is the strong mans house when controlling a society?
    - What is the strong man's possession when possessing an individual?
    - What are the strong man's possessions when controlling a society?
4. What are the two powerful tools Christ has given us to get the job done?
5. When does one receive the power of the Holy Spirit into his or her life?
6. According to Romans 10:15 and Mark 4:26-28 what special power does the gospel have?
7. According to 1 Corinthians.15:1-4 what is the heart of the gospel message?
8. What can we expect to happen when we preach the gospel along with a demonstration of the power of the Holy Spirit?
9. What two elements did Jesus often combine in the conduct of His ministry?
10. How was the power of the Holy Spirit demonstrated on the day

Chapter 4: Power Ministry and Preaching the Gospel

of Pentecost? How was the gospel proclaimed? What were the results?
11. Describe the "faith shift" that took place in the hearts of those people present on the Day of Pentecost?
12. How was the power of the Holy Spirit demonstrated by Peter and John at the Beautiful Gate? How was the gospel proclaimed? What were the results?
13. How was the power of the Holy Spirit demonstrated by Philip in Samaria? How was the gospel proclaimed? What were the results?
14. How was the power of the Holy Spirit demonstrated by Paul in the city of Lystra? How was the gospel proclaimed? What were the results?
15. According to 1 Corinthians 2:2-5, what were the two emphasis of Paul's ministry in Corinth?
16. According to 1 Corinthians 12:23-26, what should a church expect when it comes together?
17. How does Paul describe the two emphases of his apostolic ministry in Romans 15:18-20?
18. How does Paul describe His ministry to the Thessalonians in 1 Thess. 1:5?

Chapter 4: Power Ministry and Preaching the Gospel

Part II

Preparation for a Power Ministry

– CHAPTER 5 –
PREPARATION
FOR A
POWER MINISTRY

The bewildered disciples had commanded the demon to come out as they had seen Jesus do—but nothing had happened. Then, when Jesus came, He cast the demon out with a word. Later, they inquired, "Why could we not cast it out?" Jesus answered, "This kind does not go out but by prayer and fasting" (Matt. 17:21, NKJV). What is the lesson? Anyone wanting to be involved in power evangelism must give serious attention to his or her own personal resources and preparation.

In our study of power ministry, we now begin Part II, "Preparation for a Power Ministry." In this section we will closely examine the qualities and qualifications of those seeking to enter into a power ministry. In doing this we will discuss such issues as the baptism in the Holy Spirit, the gifts of the Holy Spirit, divine guidance, and spiritual weapons.

In this chapter we will answer two questions about power ministry: What are the essential elements of a power ministry? and What personal preparation is necessary for an effective power ministry?

ESSENTIAL ELEMENTS OF A POWER MINISTRY

Five elements that go into the development of an effective power ministry are anointing, faith, boldness, divine guidance, and humility. Let's examine each of these elements:

Chapter 5: Preparation for a Power Ministry

Anointing

The first essential element of a power encounter ministry is anointing. Anointing can be defined as the manifest presence of the Holy Spirit that comes upon a Spirit-filled disciple as he or she is involved in ministry. God's manifest presence should not be confused with His omnipresence, or the fact that He is everywhere at once. God's manifest presence is exhibited when His presence is comprehended by the human senses. There many are examples in the New Testament of such a manifest presence of God coming upon people enabling them to do ministry. Let's look briefly at five:

1. Peter. An anointing of the Spirit came upon Peter when he and John were called before the Jewish Sanhedrin to explain their healing of a crippled man and their of preaching the gospel in the temple court: "Then Peter, filled with the Holy Spirit, said to them … (Acts 4:8). In this instance the phrase *filled with the Holy Spirit* is not referring to Peter's initial filling with the Holy Spirit. That happened on the day of Pentecost. This was a manifest presence of the Spirit that came upon him, anointing him to speak with power and authority. It was a direct fulfillment of Jesus' prophecy in Luke 12:11-12. Don Stamps comments on this verse: "Peter received a fresh filling with the Holy Spirit that brought a sudden inspiration, wisdom and boldness by which to proclaim the truth of God."[1] In other words, Peter was anointed by the Holy Spirit.

2. The Jerusalem Congregation. Later that same day, when Peter and John reported back to the church, they all began to pray. As their prayer closed God manifested His presence again: "The place where they were meeting was shaken" (Acts 4:31). The Spirit then anointed and empowered them for the work of preaching the gospel: "And they were all filled with the Holy Spirit and spoke the word of God boldly" (Acts 4:31). In this instance an entire congregation was filled with, and empowered by, the Holy Spirit.

3. The Apostles. The anointing of the Spirit is again spoken of two verses later: "With great power the apostles continued to testify to the resurrection of the Lord Jesus, and much grace was

---

[1] Don Stamps, *The Full Life Study Bible,* KJV (Grand Rapids: Zondervan, 1992), 1663.

upon them all" (Acts 4:33). The *much grace* that was on them resulting in *great power,* was the anointing of the Holy Spirit.

4. Stephen. Luke describes Stephen is a man "full of faith and the Holy Spirit" (Acts 6:5). As a result he was anointed by the Spirit: "Now Stephen, a man full of God's grace and power, did great wonders and miraculous signs among the people ... they could not stand up against his wisdom and the Spirit by whom he spoke (vv. 8, 10). The people could even see the Spirit's anointing on his face as he spoke: "All who were sitting in the Sanhedrin looked intently at Stephen, and they saw his face was like the face of an angel" (6:15).

5. Paul. An anointing of the Holy Spirit came upon Paul on the island of Cyprus, revealing to him the judgment of God that was to fall immediately upon the sorcerer, Elymas:

> Then Saul, who was also called Paul, filled with the Holy Spirit, looked straight at Elymas and said, "You are full of all kinds of deceit and trickery. Will you never stop perverting the right ways of the Lord? Now the hand of the Lord is against you. You are going to be blind, and for a time you will be unable to see the light of the sun." Immediately darkness came over him, and he groped about, seeking someone to lead him by the hand. (Acts 13:9-11)

If one expects to minister in the power of the Spirit like these early Christians, he too must learn to walk in the Spirit and be ready to yield himself to the Spirit's promptings and control—i.e, His anointing—as He directs.

Faith

Faith is another essential element of power ministry. Faith has been defined many ways. "Faith in Christ," wrote veteran missionary Hugh Jeter, "is confidence in Christ. It is believing that He is what He says He is, and will do what He says He will do... Belief may be passive. Faith is always active."[2] "Faith," wrote another, "means that you are convinced that what God promised,

---

[2]Hugh Jeter, *By His Stripes* (Springfield, MO: Gospel Publishing House, 1977), 173.

and what you ask for, is yours; that you have received it, even before you have received it, even before you can see or feel it."

In the context of this study we will define faith as *the eagerness and ability to believe God for the miraculous.* Such faith enthusiastically looks to God to confirm His word with signs following. It is illustrated in Peter' zeal when, seeing Jesus walk on the water, he called out to Him, "Lord, if it is you tell me to come to you on the water." "Come," Jesus said. Then, Peter got down out of the boat, walked on the water and came toward Jesus (Matt. 14:28-29). Such faith can also be seen in the eagerness of Peter and John when they told the lame man to "Look at us!" (Acts 3:4). They had something he needed, and they were anxious go give it away!

The person who wants to be used in a power ministry must, as the Spirit directs, actively and eagerly seek to minister in the power and anointing of the Holy Spirit.

Boldness

Boldness is the willingness, even readiness, to take a risk of faith, even if taking a risk could mean failure and embarrassment. Such boldness is illustrated in the ministry of Paul, when, in Lystra, he risked being personally humiliated. While preaching in front of a huge crown, Paul sensed in his spirit that a certain crippled man had the faith to be healed. Paul moved with bold faith and cried out, "Stand up on your feet!" At that, the man jumped up and began to walk" (Acts 14:10).

What if the man had not walked? Paul would have been humiliated, and his ministry in Lystra would have come to an end. Paul, however, was bold in faith, willing to risk failure. As a result, a mighty revival broke out in the city. Such boldness can come only from firm commitment to God, complete confidence in His Word, and the infilling of the Holy Spirit (Acts 4:31).

Power ministry involves taking risks. We are not always guaranteed success when we minister healing or challenge demonic forces. Those who must always play it safe will never have an effective power ministry. Success will come only to those who act in faith and boldness.

Divine Guidance

Divine guidance is a third essential element in a power ministry. Before one can minister in power in any given situation, he or she must first discern the will of God in the matter, for God will never act outside of His will. The Spirit-filled minister must continually ask himself, "What is God's will in this matter? How does God want to move? What is He doing, and how may I align myself with His will?"

Jesus our example in ministry, never ministered on His own initiative. He always followed the leading of His heavenly Father. Carefully read and think about the following statements of Jesus:

> I tell you the truth, the Son can do nothing by himself; he can do only what he sees his Father doing, because whatever the Father does the Son also does. For the Father loves the Son and shows him all he does. Yes, to your amazement he will show him even greater things than these. (John 5:19-20)

> I do nothing on my own but speak just what the Father has taught me. (John 8:28)

> For I did not speak of my own accord, but the Father who sent me commanded me what to say and how to say it... So whatever I say is just what the Father has told me to say. (John 12:49-50)

Can you see that Jesus said and did only what the Father told Him to say and do? If we, like Jesus, are to minister in power, we too must be able to hear the voice of the Father and discern exactly what He is doing. We must be able to answer the questions

- What is the Father doing?
- Who does He want to heal?
- How does He want to work in this instance?
- What is my proper response to the Spirit in this situation?

These questions can only be answered by the Father Himself through the Spirit that He has given to us. We will discuss this subject more thoroughly in Chapter 9, "Divine Guidance and Power Ministry."

Chapter 5: Preparation for a Power Ministry

Someone has said, "Power ministry is easy. All you have to do is hear the voice of God and obey it." It's true. Once we discover what the Father is doing, then it is just a matter of aligning ourselves with His plans.

Humility

Humility is the ability to see ourselves as God sees us, that is, to see ourselves as we really are. This is the fifth essential ingredient of a successful power ministry. Paul was speaking of such an attitude when he said, "Do not think of yourself more highly than you ought, but rather think of yourself with sober judgment" (Rom. 12:3). He urged believers to live lives of humility, free from all pride and feelings of self-importance: "Do nothing out of selfish ambition or vain conceit, but in humility consider others better than yourselves" (Phil. 2:3).

Paul sums up this teaching on humility: "Your attitude should be the same as that of Christ Jesus…" (Phil. 2:5). He then goes on to describe the selfless attitude of Jesus:

> Who being in the very nature God, did not consider equality with God something to be grasped, but made himself nothing, taking the very nature of a servant, being made in human likeness. And being found in appearance as a man, he humbled himself and became obedient to death—even the death on a cross! (2:6-8)

Such an attitude is an essential element of any truly successful power ministry.

How our hearts have been saddened as through the years we have observed the tragic spectacle of men and women who, once mightily used of God, fell because of a prideful spirit. Forgetting the clear warnings of Scripture, they began to think too highly of themselves. They finally fell from the weight of their own self-conceit. It's true: "Pride goes before destruction, a haughty spirit before a fall" (Prov. 16:18).

I suppose that no form of ministry is more filled with the temptation to pride than a ministry of power. Power is intoxicating, and it is easy for the man or woman powerfully used of God to become drunk on what they perceive to be their own power. All

Chapter 5: Preparation for a Power Ministry

too often the crowds will assure them of their importance. Seeing the miracles they perform, the people are all too glad to treat them as if they are "gods come down to us in human form" (Acts 14:11). Money and privilege come easily, and those whom God has blessed begin to believe that the blessings of God are their due. This man or woman is ready for a great fall.

There is a second, more subtle, reason why some fall. These fall, not because their success in power ministry, but because of their lack of success. Because they so desperately want to be used of God—or because they so need to be seen by the people as someone great and powerful—they compromise the truth. Sometimes they begin to counterfeit miracles or step beyond Scripture. They are
willing to settle for an imitation rather than humbly trusting God for the reality. How sad and how tragic.

In ministry we must never forget that all the power is God's, and so is the glory. When the Seventy-two returned from their mission, they reported to Jesus, "Lord, even the demons submit to us in your name" (Luke 10:17). Jesus rejoiced with them; then He gave them a stern warning: "Do not rejoice that the spirits submit to you, but rejoice that your names are written in heaven" (v. 20). He was saying to them, "Don't become lifted up about what you have done for God, but rather rejoice in what God has done for you." Humility is an essential element of any enduring ministry in the supernatural.

PREPARATION FOR POWER ENCOUNTER MINISTRY

How must one prepare himself or herself for a power ministry? If one is sincerely wanting to be used by God in a ministry of power, he or she must address five critical issues:

Check Your Motives

First, in preparing for a power ministry one must carefully check his or her motives for wanting to be involved in such a ministry. *What* we do for God is very important; *why* we do it is even more important. One must be very sure about his motives for wanting to be used by God in a ministry of power evangelism. Simon the Sorcerer wanted a power ministry very much—but his

Chapter 5: Preparation for a Power Ministry

motives were wrong. He wanted to be seen as a man of power. He was even willing to pay money for such power. Peter, realizing his impure motives, rebuked him, telling him, "You have no part or share in this ministry, because your heart is not right before God" (Acts 8:21). How many today are also wanting a power ministry for the wrong motives?

There are both wrong and right motives for wanting to be involved in power ministry. Wrong motives include pride, desire for personal gain and advancement, and the need to exercise control over people. Right motives include a desire to glorify God, a love for and a desire to help people, and a desire to advance God's kingdom in the earth.

Strengthen Your Relationship

A second thing one must do to prepare for ministry in the supernatural is to strengthen his or her relationship with God. One can truly minister only out of an authentic relationship with God. One's ministry *for* God will never be stronger than his or her bond *with* Him. As we have seen earlier in this chapter, Jesus Himself ministered out of His relationship with the Father. Remember His words: "The Father loves the Son and shows him all he does" (John 5:20). It was out of this loving relationship with His Father that Jesus' ministry flowed.

In like manner, the apostles ministered out of their relationship with Christ. The Bible notes that the people "took note that these men had been with Jesus" (Acts 4:13). Anyone wanting to be used by God in a ministry of power evangelism must, like Jesus and the apostles, spend much time in secret prayer, strengthening their relationship with God. Scripture reading, meditation, and submission to His will are also necessary to build a strong relationship with God.

Increase Your Understanding

A third way to prepare oneself for ministry in the supernatural is to increase one's understanding of the subject. Reading and applying the principles in this book is a good first step. However, it is just the beginning. Here are two other ways one can increase his or her understanding of a scriptural ministry of power:

Chapter 5: Preparation for a Power Ministry

1. Read the gospels and Acts. This author can testify from personal experience that a thorough and systematic reading—and rereading, and rereading—of the gospels and Acts can change one's life. It has his. Once an old minister who had been greatly used in a ministry of healing and casting out demons was asked by a young minister, "Can you recommend to me any good books on the subject of divine healing?" "Yes," said the old man, "I can recommend four wonderful books." At that, they young man pulled out his pen and a pad of paper. "What are these four wonderful books?" he asked, "I must have them." The old preacher answered, "Matthew, Mark, Luke, and John." Make it your practice to read and reread the four Gospels and Acts many times, constantly asking yourself such questions as, "How did Jesus and the apostles minister in power? How did they heal the sick and cast out devils? What were the secrets of their success? How may I imitate their lives and ministries?"

2. Read good books on the subject. Of course you may also read books on the subject by reputable and respected men and women of God. But beware, not every book published on this subject is based on sound biblical principles, nor are their authors always men of integrity and honor.

Submit to God's Will

Fourth, one must prepare himself or herself for power ministry by submitting totally to the will of God. Jesus submitted Himself absolutely to the will of His heavenly Father, and thus received His Father's blessing. We too, if we are to receive the God's blessing, must submit ourselves totally to His will. We must never forget: God will only anoint *His* plans, and He has promised only to confirm *His* word, not ours, with signs following (Mark 16:15-20).

Get Experience

Finally, if one intends to be involved in a power ministry, he or she must acquire the necessary experience. This includes both spiritual and practical experience.

1. Spiritual Experience. Spiritual experience must include being born again (John 3:3-7). The Bible tells the story of certain men who attempted power ministry without ever having been born again:

Chapter 5: Preparation for a Power Ministry

> Some Jews who went around driving out evil spirits tried to invoke the name of the Lord Jesus over those who were demon-possessed. They would say, "In the name of Jesus, whom Paul preaches, I command you to come out." Seven sons of Sceva, a Jewish chief priest, were doing this. One day the evil spirit answered them, "Jesus I know, and I know about Paul, but who are you?" Then the man who had the evil spirit jumped on them and overpowered them all. He gave the such a beating that they ran out of the house naked and bleeding. (Acts 19:13-16)

Let this story serve as a warning to those who would be involved in power ministry without ever being born again.

Next, in order to minister in power one must be filled with the Spirit as were the first-century disciples (Acts 2:4). The baptism in the Holy Spirit was the early church's source of spiritual dynamic and power, and it remains our source of spiritual power today. We will discuss this powerful experience at length in the next chapter, "The Baptism in the Holy Spirit and Power Ministry."

2. Practical Experience. As with any other job, competence in power ministry is gained through practical experience. The person wanting to become competent in this area of ministry must do so through practical field experience. This experience is best gained in working with an experienced minister. This is how the Twelve, under the guidance of Jesus, gained practical experience. As we participate in power ministry, we will experience both successes and failures. In this way we will learn to more effectively minister for Christ.

In summary, anyone desiring to be used in power ministry must give serious attention to his or her own personal preparation. We must never forget that we minister, not out of our own strength and resources, but out of the strength and resources that come from God.

FOR REFLECTION AND REVIEW

1. What is meant by the phrase the anointing?
2. List five examples from the book of Acts of when the anointing came up on believers.

Chapter 5: Preparation for a Power Ministry

3. How are we defining faith this course? How are Peter and John examples of this kind of faith?
4. Define boldness.
5. Explain why boldness is necessary in power encounter ministry.
6. What four questions must one be able to answer before he or she can have an effective power ministry?
7. Why is divine guidance so necessary in power ministry?
8. How did Jesus seek His Father's guidance in His ministry?
9. Define humility and tell why it is so important in a power ministry.
10. Discuss two things that may cause individuals involved in power ministry to fall.
11. List five essential elements of a power ministry.
12. What are some wrong motives for wanting to be used in a ministry of power?
13. What are some right motives for wanting to be used in a ministry of power?
14. Why is it important that one who wants to be used in a ministry of power strengthen his or her relationship with God?
15. How can one strengthen his or her relationship with God?
16. Discuss three ways one can increase his or her understanding of power encounter ministry.
17. Why is submission to God's will important to a power encounter ministry?
18. What two spiritual experiences are necessary prerequisites for a power ministry?
19. List four things one must do in preparation for a power ministry.

Chapter 5: Preparation for a Power Ministry

– Chapter 6 –

The Baptism in the Holy Spirit and Power Encounter

Before one can be truly effective in power ministry, he or she must understand and experience the baptism in the Holy Spirit. This is the normative experience for believers (both in the New Testament and today), and is our source of spiritual power for life and ministry. In this lesson we will examine this essential Christian experience.

THE BAPTISM IN THE HOLY SPIRIT DEFINED

The baptism in the Holy Spirit can be described in many ways. By way of definition, we will mention five:

A Key Goal of Christ's Mission

One key goal of Christ's earthly mission was to baptize His followers in the Holy Spirit. From the beginning, Jesus' plan was not just to win a local following, no matter how large or how impressive it might be to human observers. His plan was to conquer the world, and He would use people to do it. These individuals must be well trained and well equipped. An essential piece of equipment He would give them was the power of the Holy Spirit. At the onset of Jesus' ministry, John the Baptist announced, "The man on whom you see the Spirit come down and remain, is he who will baptize you with the Holy Spirit" (John 1:33). From

Chapter 6: The Baptism in the Holy Spirit and Power Ministry

the very beginning Jesus intended to baptize his followers with the Holy Spirit. It was a key goal of His ministry.

An Immersion and a Filling

The baptism in the Holy Spirit can be characterized as both an immersion in, and a filling with, the Holy Spirit. Jesus called the experience a baptism, or an immersion, in the Holy Spirit:

> Do not leave Jerusalem, but wait for the gift my Father promised, which you have heard me speak about. For John baptized with water, but in a few days you will be baptized with [immersed in] the Holy Spirit. (Acts 1:4-5)

Seven days later, on the Day of Pentecost, the Spirit came. The Bible describes the disciples' experience on that day as a filling with the Spirit: "All of them were filled with the Holy Spirit and began to speak in other tongues as the Spirit enabled them" (Acts 2:4).

Just as an opened container can, at the same time, be both immersed in and filled with water, so it was for these believers on the Day of Pentecost. So it can be for us today.

Separate from Regeneration.

The baptism in the Holy Spirit does not occur at regeneration, as some have taught. It is an experience with the Spirit distinct and separate from this initial experience of the Christian life. Just as the Samaritans (Acts 8:12-14), Paul (9:3-18), and the Ephesians (19:1-7) were first born again, and later "received the Holy Spirit" (Acts 8:17), so it is with us today. The baptism in the Holy Spirit is an experience with the Holy Spirit distinct and separate from the new birth. It's purpose is to empower believers to be witnesses for Christ (Acts 1:8).

Reader, have you been born again? Are you a true child of God? If you are not, then receive Christ today. If you are, then you should ask God to fill you with the Holy Spirit as He did the believers of the first-century church (Luke 11:9-13; Acts 2:1-4).

A Clothing with Power

Jesus described the baptism in the Holy Spirit as a clothing with power: "I am going to send you what my Father has promised; but stay in the city until you have been clothed with power from on high" (Luke 24:49).

Here, Jesus paints a picture of a person being clothed with the power of God, and once clothed, that person is ready to do the works of God. Jesus promised such power to His followers after the Holy Spirit had come upon them: "But you will receive power when the Holy Spirit comes upon you" (Acts 1:8).

The Greek word here translated "comes upon" (*eperchomai*) is the same word used in Luke 1:35 to describe the Holy Spirit coming upon Mary at the conception of Jesus: "The Holy Spirit will come upon you, and the power of the Most High will overshadow you." The picture is, as in Acts 1:8, of one's being totally wrapped in, and overwhelmed by, the power of God. That is what happens when a believer is baptized in the Holy Spirit.

A Promise for All Believers

Every believer can, and should, be baptized in the Holy Spirit. The Bible says that the 120 who gathered on the Day of Pentecost "were *all* filled with the Holy Spirit" (Acts 2:4, emphasis added). It does not say that 119 were filled, and one was not. It says they were *all* filled. From the very beginning God wanted us to know His will concerning the baptism in the Holy Spirit. It is His will that every believer be filled with the Spirit.

Peter made this point clear when, standing up on the Day of Pentecost, he spoke about this wonderful gift: "The promise is for you and your children and for *all* who are far off—for *all* whom the Lord our God will call" (Acts 2:39, emphasis added, see also 2:17-18).

The promise of the baptism in the Holy Spirit, and the power it brings, is for "all whom the Lord our God will call." That means, my friend, that the promise is for you too. Will you call on the Lord today, and ask Him to fill you with His precious Holy Spirit?

Chapter 6: The Baptism in the Holy Spirit and Power Ministry

THE IMPORTANCE OF THE BAPTISM IN THE HOLY SPIRIT TO A POWER MINISTRY

Although it seems almost too obvious to mention, we will say it just the same: before entering into a ministry of power evangelism, one should first be empowered by the Holy Spirit. This empowering for ministry comes with the baptism in this Holy Spirit, as we have been discussing (Acts 1:8). The importance of this experience to a power encounter ministry is demonstrated in two dramatic ways:

Commanded in Scripture

First, the importance of the baptism in the Holy Spirit is demonstrated by the fact that it is commanded in Scripture.

1. Commanded by Jesus. In His final word to His disciples Jesus solemnly commanded them to be baptized in the Holy Spirit (Acts 1:4-5). During the forty days after His resurrection, He repeatedly instructed them not to begin witnessing until they were baptized in the Holy Spirit (Luke 24:49; Acts 1:8). Jesus was fully aware that the ministry to which He had called His disciples was far beyond their human capabilities. They, therefore, must not attempt it in their own power. They must first be "clothed with the power from on high."

2. Commanded by Paul. In his letter to the Ephesian Christians, Paul gave two commands. They were expected to obey both: "Do not be drunk with wine, in which is dissipation; but be filled with the Spirit" (Eph. 5:18, NKJV). We, too, must be filled with the Spirit. Before we attempt to enter into any ministry—much less a ministry of power—we must be empowered by the Holy Spirit. How foolish we would be to think otherwise!

Our Source of Power

The importance of the baptism in the Holy Spirit to a power ministry is also demonstrated by the fact that the Holy Spirit is our source of power for such a ministry. It was so for both Jesus and the early church, and it is so for us today.

1. Jesus' source of power. Jesus' power for ministry came through His anointing with the Holy Spirit. That anointing first occurred at His baptism (Luke 4:22). It was not until after He had

Chapter 6: The Baptism in the Holy Spirit and Power Ministry

been anointed by the Holy Spirit that He entered into His messianic ministry. Peter declared that "God anointed Jesus of Nazareth with the Holy Spirit and power, and ... he went around doing good and healing all who were under the power of the devil, because God was with him" (Acts 10:38).

Although Jesus was, is, and never ceased to be, the eternal Son of God, while He was here on earth, He chose to minister in the Spirit's power. He did this so that He might establish a pattern of ministry for us to follow (John 14:12-16).

It is interesting to note that Jesus never healed one sick person, never cast out one demon, and never performed even one miracle until He was first anointed by the Holy Spirit at His baptism. After His anointing, however, He at once began to move and minister in power (Luke 3:22-23). A careful reading of the following series of verses from the gospel of Luke will demonstrate this fact: Luke 4:1-2; 4:14; 18-21; 5:17; 6:19. If such an anointing of the Spirit was essential for Jesus in the performance of His ministry, how much more is it for us today!

2. The early church's source of power. It is clear from an honest reading of the book of Acts that the baptism in the Holy Spirit was essential to the ministry of the New Testament church. Acts repeatedly emphasizes that the baptism in the Spirit was God's primary provision for ministry. This provision was given so that the church might continue the ministry of Jesus, and so that it might be able to fulfill its mission of carrying the gospel to the ends of the earth (Acts 1:8).

On several occasions in the Acts we are told of people being baptized in, or filled with, the Spirit (Acts 2:4; 4:33; 8:17; 9:17-18; 10:44-46; 19:6). Powerful anointed preaching and dramatic demonstrations of God's power followed each of these outpourings. As a result, a great many people came to the Lord. These powerful fillings with the Spirit were the source of the church's miraculous power. It was after one such outpouring of the Spirit that "with great power the apostles continued to testify to the resurrection of the Lord Jesus, and much grace was upon them all" (Acts 4:33).

This same power is available to us today if we, like them, will be filled with the Spirit.

Chapter 6: The Baptism in the Holy Spirit and Power Ministry

HOW YOU CAN RECEIVE THE HOLY SPIRIT TODAY

The question arises, "How can one be baptized in the Holy Spirit today?" We will now answer this important question. It is our hope that after reading these instructions you will personally receive this promised gift.

Preconditions for Receiving

There are three preconditions for being baptized in, or filled with, the Holy Spirit. Before one can be filled with the Spirit he or she must be truly born again, have a sincere desire to be filled with the Spirit, and be willing to obey God and share Christ with others. Let's look briefly at each of these preconditions:

1. Be truly born again. The Bible teaches that before one can be baptized in the Holy Spirit he or she must be truly born again. Jesus spoke of "the Spirit of truth, whom the world cannot receive, because it neither sees Him nor knows Him" (John 14:17, NKJV). Only those who have been truly born of the Spirit of God are candidates to be filled with the Holy Spirit (Acts 2:38-39). This new birth experience involves personal faith in Jesus Christ as Savior, the complete surrender of one's will to the will of God, and repentance, which is turning from anything that offends God. Have you been truly born again? If not, why not turn to Christ right now in faith and repentance?

2. Desire to be filled. A second precondition for being filled with the Spirit is a desire to be filled. Jesus said, "Blessed are those who hunger and thirst after righteousness, for they will be filled" (Matt. 5:6). Filled with what? Filled with the righteousness of God that comes only through the sanctifying power of the Spirit (1 Cor. 6:11, Rom. 16:15). To be filled with the Spirit one must desire God more than anything else. Jesus once said, "If anyone is thirsty, let him come to me and drink." (John 7:37). Are you thirsty for more of God? If so, you have met the second precondition for being filled with the Spirit.

3. Willingness to Obey the Great Commission. A third precondition for being filled with the Spirit is willingness to obey Christ's command to preach the gospel to the lost. When the Jewish leaders commanded Peter and John to stop preaching the gospel, Peter replied, "We must obey God rather than men!" (Acts

Chapter 6: The Baptism in the Holy Spirit and Power Ministry

5:29). Then he told them, "We are witnesses of these things, and so is the Holy Spirit, whom God has given to those who obey him" (v. 32). God is anxious to give His Spirit to anyone who will obey Christ's command to preach the gospel to the lost.

How to Receive the Spirit

If you have met the foregoing preconditions, you can be filled with the Spirit right now. Just do the following:

1. Approach God's throne with confidence. When you come to be filled with the Spirit, you should come boldly before God. The Scriptures encourage us, "Let us then approach the throne of grace with confidence" (Heb. 4:16). We can come before God without fear because we know we are coming according to His perfect will (1 John 5:14). Therefore, when you come to be filled with the Spirit, come in boldness and faith, knowing that God warmly welcomes you into His presence.

2. Sincerely ask God to fill you. Jesus has given us wonderful promises concerning the Holy Spirit. He said, "Ask and it will be given to you" (Luke 11:9). And again, "Everyone who asks receives" (v. 10). What a wonderful promise—*everyone* who asks receives! Jesus also promised, "If you then, though you are evil, know how to give good gifts to your children, how much more will your Father in heaven give the Holy Spirit to those who ask him!" (v 13). Do you want God to fill you with His Spirit today? Just ask Him; He is ready. If you are sensitive to the Lord, when you ask, you will sense the Spirit's presence coming upon you.

3. Receive by faith. As with any of God's provisions, the baptism in the Holy Spirit is appropriated by faith (Gal. 3:14). This is not a passive faith that sits and waits on God to move. It is an aggressive faith that reaches out and takes what God has graciously offered. Jesus gave us a key for receiving the Holy Spirit when He said, "Therefore I tell you, whatever you ask for in prayer, believe that you have received it, and it will be yours" (Mark 11:24). Ask God for the Holy Spirit, expecting Him to immediately fill you. Then, by an act of faith, believe that you *have* received. The instant you believe, the Spirit will come and fill you. You will sense a fullness of His Presence deep within.

4. Speak in faith. Once you sense the Spirit's presence inside, speak! Not from your mind, but from your spirit, from your "innermost being," where you feel His presence (see 1 Cor. 14:14-15). As you speak out in faith, and as you yield yourself completely to God, you will begin to speak in tongues as the Spirit gives the words (Acts 2:4; 10:46; 19:6). As Jesus promised, "rivers of living water" will flow from your innermost being" (John 7:38).

Evidences of Receiving
Once you have been filled with the Spirit, you will never be the same. You can expect certain "evidences" to follow your infilling.

1. The initial evidence. The first evidence of your receiving the Holy Spirit will be speaking in other tongues as the Spirit enables you. This was the recurring evidence experienced by believers in the book of Acts, and is the initial physical evidence of being baptized in the Holy Spirit. Read it for yourself in your own Bible in Acts 2:1-4; 10:45-47; and 19:1-6. Speaking in tongues is a sign from God that He has empowered you to be His witness (Acts 1:8; 2:4).

2. Power to witness. While speaking in tongues is the initial sign that one has been baptized in the Holy Spirit, power to witness is the primary purpose of the experience. Jesus said, "You will receive power when the Holy Spirit comes upon you and you will be my witnesses..." (Acts 1:8). With the infilling of the Spirit comes a deep desire and the necessary power to share Christ with the lost at home and around the world.

3. Other scriptural evidences relating to power ministry. As you learn to walk in the Spirit many other evidences will follow. Below are listed seven that apply directly to a ministry of power evangelism:

- Boldness (Acts 2:14-41; 4:31)
- Power to do the works of Jesus (John 14:16-18; 16:14)
- The manifestation of various gifts of the Spirit (1 Cor. 12:1-11)
- An increased sensitivity to sin that grieves the Holy Spirit (John 16:7-11)
- A greater desire and ability to pray and to intercede for others (Rom. 8:28-29)
- An increased awareness of God's presence in one's life

Chapter 6: The Baptism in the Holy Spirit and Power Ministry

(John 14:16-18)
- A greater love for God and for people (Rom. 5:5).

The power of the Spirit is essential to any power ministry. This power is given when one is baptized in the Holy Spirit. It is essential, therefore, that any believer wanting to be used by God in the area of power evangelism be baptized in the Holy Spirit. If you have not been baptized in the Holy Spirit, you should begin seeking to be filled right now by asking God to fill you with His Spirit.

FOR REFLECTION AND REVIEW

1. Why do we say that the baptism in the Holy Spirit was a key goal of Christ's mission on earth?
2. What do we mean when we say that the baptism in the Holy Spirit is both an "immersion in" and a "filling with" the Holy Spirit?
3. Cite three biblical examples proving that the baptism in the Holy Spirit is an experience distinct and separate from the experience of regeneration.
4. Why do we say that the baptism in the Holy Spirit is a promise for all believers?
5. Cite two New Testament texts commanding believers to be filled with the Holy Spirit.
6. By what power did Jesus perform miracles? Explain your answer.
7. What was the source of power for the New Testament church? How did they receive this power?
8. State two reasons why we say that the baptism in the Holy Spirit is essential for a power ministry.
9. Why do we say that before a person can be baptized in the Holy Spirit he or she must first be born again?
10. What do we mean when we say a person must have a desire to be filled before he or she can receive the Holy Spirit?
11. State two preconditions for being filled with the Holy Spirit.
12. What is the first thing one must do to be filled with the Holy Spirit?
13. When one comes to be filled with the Spirit, how should he or she approach God?

Chapter 6: The Baptism in the Holy Spirit and Power Ministry

14. What do we mean when we say that one should "speak in faith" when receiving the Holy Spirit?
15. What the initial physical evidence can one expect when he or she is filled with the Holy Spirit?
16. According to Jesus, what is the primary purpose of the baptism in the Holy Spirit?
17. List seven other evidences of being filled with the Spirit that relate directly to power ministry.

– CHAPTER 7 –

SPIRITUAL GIFTS
AND POWER ENCOUNTER

An understanding of spiritual gifts, especially the nine "manifestation" gifts listed in 1 Corinthians 12:8-10, is essential to a power encounter ministry. It is largely through the operation of these gifts that power ministry is released. By means of these gifts Jesus and the apostles healed the sick, cast out demons, and performed their miraculous works. The same is true today, through the release of spiritual gifts we can do the same works as did Jesus and the early believers (John 14:12).

Anyone wanting to be used in a ministry of power must have a thorough understanding of these gifts and how they operate in the life of a Spirit-filled believer. In this chapter we will introduce these gifts and talk about their role in power ministry.

SPIRITUAL GIFTS DEFINED

Gifts Defined

Spiritual gifts have been defined in various ways. For our purposes in this study we will use the following definition: *Spiritual gifts are supernatural anointings released through Spirit-filled believers by the Holy Spirit to accomplish the will of the Father.*

Gifts Explained

Let's examine the above definition more closely by looking at it phrase by phrase:

Supernatural anointings. Spiritual gifts are supernatural anointings. In other words, they have their origin, not in the abilities of man, but in the Spirit of God. They come as "anointings," and are administered under the impulse and direction of the Holy Spirit. They are released as the Spirit moves upon and through yielded individuals.

Released through Spirit-filled believers. Spiritual gifts are truly gifts. They are, therefore, distributed, not on the basis of merit or reward, but as simple demonstrations of God's free grace. They are not, however, given as personal possessions, but are released *through* yielded believers on a case-by-case basis to meet specific needs in relation to the work of God. "Spirit-filled believers" are those Christians who have been baptized in the Holy Spirit and are currently walking and living in step with the Spirit (Acts 2:4, Gal. 5:25).

By the Holy Spirit. Spiritual gifts are released by the Holy Spirit. The Spirit of God is the divine Dispenser of the gifts (1 Cor. 12:4-6). They operate, therefore, not according to the will of man, but according to the will of the Spirit (1 Cor. 12:11).

To accomplish the will of the Father. The reason the gifts are released is to accomplish the will of the Father. They are not given to fulfill the plans and desires of any person. They are given to accomplish God's will, edify the church, and to advance His kingdom in the earth.

Spiritual Gifts Identified

While we recognize that there are other listings of spiritual gifts in Paul's letters (see Rom. 12:6-8; 1 Cor. 12:28, 29-30; Eph. 4:11), we also believe that these nine manifestations (Greek: *phanerosis*) have a special place in power evangelism. Paul wrote,

> Now to each one the manifestation of the Spirit is given for the common good. To one there is given through the Spirit the message of wisdom, to another the message of knowledge by means of the same Spirit, to another faith by the same Spirit, to another gifts of healing by that one Spirit, to another miraculous powers, to another prophecy, to another distinguishing between spirits, to another speaking in different kinds of tongues, and to still another the interpretation of tongues. (1 Cor. 12:7-10)

Chapter 7: Spiritual Gifts and Power Encounter

These nine gifts seem to fall naturally into three groupings. The first grouping we call "revelation gifts." These revelation gifts are given *that we might know the mind of God.* They are the "word of knowledge," the "word of wisdom," and the "discerning of spirits." The second grouping we call "prophetic gifts." These are given *that we might speak the words of God.* These gifts include the gift of "prophecy," the gift of "tongues," and the "interpretation of tongues." The third grouping we call "power gifts." They are given *that we might do the works of God.* These are "gifts of healings," the gift of "faith," and "miraculous powers" (or "works of power"). We define these gifts as follows:

Revelation Gifts
(Given to know the mind of God)

- *Word (message) of knowledge:* A Spirit-conferred revelation of a portion of God's knowledge
- *Word (message) of wisdom* A Spirit-conferred revelation of a portion of God's wisdom
- *Distinguishing between spirits:* A Spirit-conferred revelation of what S[s]pirit is being manifested or motivating an action

---

Prophetic Gifts
(Given to say the words of God)

- *Gift of prophecy* A Spirit-inspired speaking forth of a message from God
- *Different kinds of tongues* A Spirit-inspired speaking forth of a message from God, or a prayer to God, in a language not known to the speaker
- *Interpretation of tongues:* A Spirit-inspired speaking forth of the meaning of a message or prayer spoken in tongues

Power Gifts
(Given to do the works of God)

- *Gift of faith* — A Spirit-energized surge of faith to accomplish a God-ordained task
- *Gifts of healing* — A Spirit-energized healing of diseases and infirmities
- *Miraculous powers*[1] — A Spirit-energized release of divine power to accomplish a special work of God.

SPIRITUAL GIFTS AND POWER ENCOUNTER

Let's now discuss how these various gifts relate to a power encounter ministry.

Revelation Gifts and Power Encounter

The revelation gifts are essential to a ministry of power. In Acts a word of knowledge or a discerning of spirits often began a chain of events leading to the release of a power gift (see 14:8-10; 16:16-18).

Before we can do the works of God, we must first know the mind of God. That is, we must know what the will of God is in a given matter. Jesus did not travel around randomly healing sick people. He first heard from His heavenly Father, then He did as the Father directed. Listen to His words: "Most assuredly, I say to you, the Son can do nothing of Himself, but what He sees the Father do; for whatever He does, the Son also does in like manner" (John 5:19). Jesus did nothing without first determining the Father's will concerning the matter. Likewise, it is essential that we, too, receive revelation of God's will concerning a given matter. Such revelation is often received through words of knowledge.

---

[1] This gift could more properly be called "works of power" or literally from the Greek (*energemata dunameon*) "operations of works of power."

It is also often crucial that the gift of discerning of spirits be exercised before we know how to approach a healing encounter. We must determine not only if a person is sick, but *why* he is sick. Is the sickness caused by natural causes or is it caused by demonic affliction? The story is told of the British evangelist, Smith Wigglesworth. Once he was praying for two deaf men. To the first he said, "Be healed!" and the man was immediately healed. To the next he said, "Come out of this man you spirit of deafness." This man's ears were also immediately opened. Later, when asked why he dealt with each man differently he replied, "You don't heal demons; you cast them out." Mr. Wigglesworth would not have known how to properly minister to each person without the operation of the gift of discerning of spirits. How often do we try to "heal demons" and "cast out illnesses," when we should be doing just the opposite? The release of revelation gifts often sets the stage for the release of power gifts to follow.

Prophetic Gifts and Power Encounter

The prophetic gifts are an indispensable part of power evangelism. A prophetic gift will often precede or follow a demonstration of God's power. It was so on the Day of Pentecost when Peter preached his famous Pentecost "sermon." Actually, this sermon was not a sermon at all, at least not in the traditional sense, but a prophetic utterance spoken under a powerful anointing of the Holy Spirit.[2] As a result of seeing and hearing the miracles of Pentecost (power encounter), and hearing the prophetic utterance of Peter (truth encounter), the people were deeply convicted of their sins and 3,000 were saved and baptized that very day (Acts 2:37, 41).

Paul taught in 1 Corinthians 14:22 that speaking in tongues is a sign to unbelievers that God is at work in the gathering of Christians. He also says that through prophecy the sinner can be made aware of the presence of God. As a result he will be convinced "that he is a sinner ... and the secrets of his heart will be laid bare. So he will fall down and worship God" (vv. 24-25). The

---

[2]Stanley Horton, *What the Bible Says About the Holy Spirit* (Springfield, MO: Gospel Publishing House, 1976), 144.

fulfillment of predictive prophecy as used by the New Testament prophet, Agabus, can also serve as a powerful witness to the presence of God in the church (Acts 11:27ff; 21:10ff).

Power Gifts and Power Encounter

Power gifts represent the most obvious use of the gifts of the Spirit in power evangelism. Through the release of the gifts of healing and faith, people are healed, God's power and presence are demonstrated, sinners are brought face to face with the reality of a living God, and hearts are prepared to receive the gospel. In the healing of Aeneas such a thing happened:

> As Peter traveled about the country, he went to visit the saints in Lydda. There he found a man named Aeneas, a paralytic who had been bedridden for eight years. 'Aeneas,' Peter said to him, 'Jesus Christ heals you. Get up and take care of your mat.' Immediately Aeneas got up. All those who lived in Lydda and Sharon saw him and turned to the Lord. (Acts 9:32-35)

Thus, through the release of a gift of healing, a great revival was sparked in an entire region.

Another power gift essential to power ministry is the gift of miraculous powers (or more literally "operations of works of power"). The operation of this gift seems to include a divine release of power to effect healing and other miraculous results (Luke 5:17; 6:19; Mark 5:30). According to Bible commentator Don Stamps,

> They include divine acts in which God's kingdom is manifested against Satan and evil spirits ... including the casting out of demons."[3] (See also Luke 11:20.)

RELEASING SPIRITUAL GIFTS

The question arises, "How may one be used in the gifts of the

---

[3] Don Stamps, "Spiritual Gifts for Believers" in *The Full Life Study Bible,* KJV (Grand Rapids: Zondervan, 1992), 1790.

Chapter 7: Spiritual Gifts and Power Encounter

Holy Spirit?" Earlier we said that the gifts come as anointings from God. It is, therefore, the responsibility of the Spirit-filled disciple to learn to walk in the Spirit and to yield to the Spirit as He prompts. With this in mind, we will address two important questions concerning the release of the spiritual gifts in ministry:

1. How does the anointing come? God anoints us and gives us His Spirit as we walk in obedience to His will and to His commands. Peter testified that the Spirit (i.e., the anointing to minister; see context) is "given to those who obey" (Acts 5:32). In other words, the anointing comes at the point of obedience. Take for example the anointing to understand the Word of God (John 16:13; 1 John 2:20, 27). It comes only as we obey God and begin to prayerfully read and study the Word. As we do, the Holy Spirit comes to illuminate the Scriptures to us.

Likewise, the Holy Spirit will anoint us in prayer. Paul said that He will come and pray through us "with groans that words cannot express" (Rom. 8:26). However, before the Spirit can anoint our prayer, we must first take the step of obedience and begin to pray! At that point, if we will open out hearts to Him, he will come, fill us, and begin to pray through us.

In much the same way, the Spirit will anoint us to witness (Acts 1:8). The anointing comes only at the point of obedience, not before. We must first, in obedience to God, take the initiative and begin to witness to someone. Then, the anointing will come to empower and enable us.

The same is true in ministering spiritual gifts. The Holy Spirit may prompt us to speak a prophetic word or minister healing to a sick person. As we obey His voice, and begin to minister, God sends His Spirit to fill and anoint us, enabling us to do that ministry. He will release through us the gift, or gifts, needed to accomplish the work. If, however, we refuse to obey His word, and ignore the promptings of His Spirit, the anointing subsides. The principle is this: the anointing comes a the point of obedience.

2. How is the anointing released? Once the anointing comes, the spiritual gift must then be released by an act of faith. Faith acts like a switch that releases the anointing and discharges the gift. Just as a switch releases the potential energy in the electrical wires, faith releases the anointing to accomplish the work of God.

This is what happened to Peter at the Beautiful Gate. He acted in bold faith by commanding the lame man to walk and taking him by the hand and lifting him up (Acts 3:6). At that instant, a gift of healing was released causing the mans feet and ankles to become strong. The same thing happened to Paul when he commanded the lame man in Lystra to stand up on his feet (Acts 14:9).

When the Holy Spirit wants a work to be done, He will often direct a Spirit-filled disciple to do it. As the disciple obeys, the Holy Spirit comes upon him and fills him. Then, as the Spirit prompts, the disciple must act in bold faith. This act of faith could be to speak a word or take an action. When the disciple acts in faith, the anointing is released, the gift is manifested, and the work is accomplished.

Gifts of the Spirit are enablements God has given to us that He may work His works through us. They are essential equipment for power ministry. We must each make it our aim to understand these powerful manifestations of the Holy Spirit, and we must know how to release them in ministry.

FOR REFLECTION AND REVIEW

1. What do we mean when we say spiritual gifts are "supernatural anointings?"
2. When we say spiritual gifts are "given to Spirit-filled believers," who are we talking about?
3. Who is the source of all spiritual gifts?
4. What is the purpose of spiritual gifts?
5. Name the three revelation gifts. Why are they given?
6. Name the three prophetic gifts. Why are they given?
7. Name the three power gifts. For what purpose are they given?
8. Why are the revelation gifts important in power ministry?
9. How can the prophetic gifts be used in a power ministry?
10. List the three power gifts and tell how they are used in power evangelism.
11. How are spiritual gifts released in ministry? What is the role of obedience? What is the role faith?

– Chapter 8 –

Pastoring
the
Spiritual Gifts

A true Pentecostal pastor wants to see the gifts of the Spirit in operation his or her church. He longs for the power of God to be released during the services. He wants to see God glorified and the needs of people met. To do this, he must learn how to properly "pastor" the spiritual gifts. This demands two skills: First, a pastor must be able to encourage the use of spiritual gifts in his church. Next, he must know how to prevent their misuse.

ENCOURAGING THE USE OF SPIRITUAL GIFTS

A pastor can encourage the operation of spiritual gifts in his or her church in several ways. Let's look at five of these ways:

Accepting Pastoral Responsibility
The pastor is responsible to ensure that spiritual gifts are in operation in his or her church. This is one responsibility he cannot delegate to others. He must, therefore, eagerly accept it. As God's appointed leader of the congregation, the pastor must make the operation of spiritual gifts one of his chief ministry goals. A careful reading of 1 Corinthians 12 to 14 reveals the damage that the misuse of spiritual gifts can bring to a church. It also reveals the blessings brought by the proper use of the gifts. This contrast is demonstrated in Figure 8:1 below:

Chapter 8: Pastoring the Spiritual Gifts

Figure 8.1
Comparing the Outcomes of the Misuse and Proper Use of Spiritual Gifts

Damage that will result if a pastor allows the misuse of spiritual gifts:	Blessings that will come if a pastor ensures the proper use of spiritual gifts:
1. The people will remain ignorant (12:1; 14:38).	1. The church will be taught and built up (12:7; 14:4, 5, 6, 12, 19, 26).
2. Divisions will be created in the body (12:25).	2. The church will be unified, strengthened, encouraged and comforted (12:12; 14:3, 31).
3. Confusion will result (14:33).	3. Peace will result (14:33; 40).
4. Only one gift will be used over and over, to the exclusion of all others (14:27-28).	4. All of the gifts will be allowed to operate (12:7-11, 25, 27-31; 14:26).
5. The church's witness to the world will become a "clanging cymbal" (13:1).	5. The church will get ready for battle (14:8).
6. Visitors will say that "you are out of your mind" (14:23).	6. Visitors will say, "Amen! God is really among you" (14:16, 25).
7. The lost will be driven away (14:23, 33).	7. Souls will be won to Christ (14:24–25).

Chapter 8: Pastoring the Spiritual Gifts

Training Believers

A pastor can encourage the use of spiritual gifts in the church through systematic teaching. His or her teaching should include instruction about what the gifts are, their proper use, and how they can be released in ministry. The pastor could teach a Sunday School class or a special seminar on the subject. The training methods may vary; however, the pastor must be careful to teach only what the Bible says about spiritual gifts and their operation in the church.

Modeling the Use of Spiritual Gifts

A pastor must do more than tell his people about spiritual gifts, he must also *show* them how the gifts operate in his own life. This is a great responsibility. The pastor must himself "eagerly desire" spiritual gifts (1 Cor. 12:31). Only in this way will he be able to model the operation of the gifts. This means he must seek God until the Holy Spirit uses him in the ministry of spiritual gifts.

Pastor, do spiritual gifts operate freely and biblically in your church? If not, then God wants to begin with you in manifesting spiritual gifts in your congregation!

Encouraging Believers to Exercise Spiritual Gifts

A pastor should seek to create a desire for spiritual gifts in his or her people. He can show how their lives can be blessed as they begin to be used by God in this area. As they exercise spiritual gifts, the church will be blessed and strengthened.

The surrounding community will also be blessed. As the church demonstrates the power and compassion of God through spiritual gifts, sick people will be healed, broken marriages will be mended, and those who are possessed by demons will be delivered. Best of all, people will be saved as the Spirit uses God's people to minister through them.

Spiritual gifts operate best in a non-threatening atmosphere. The people must not fear being rebuked or criticized every time they attempt to release a spiritual gift. If they are criticized often, they will hesitate or refuse to respond to the Spirit. A pastor must give his people the time and opportunity to learn how to use spiritual gifts. At times people will make mistakes. Their pastor should expect this; mistakes are a normal part of the learning process. When they do make mistakes, he should gently and kindly correct them. The pastor should remind them what the Bible says about the proper use of spiritual gifts. Most importantly, the pastor should encourage his people to keep trying.

Spiritual gifts operate best when God's presence can be strongly felt. We can create such an atmosphere through sincere prayer and Spirit-directed worship. We should be open to the Spirit of God at all times in our church services.

Allowing Time in the Church Service

Some pastors never see spiritual gifts in operation in their church. This may be because they never give the Holy Spirit the time or opportunity to manifest His presence through the gifts. Such pastors are too busy talking, singing, and making announcements. They do not give the church time to wait upon God during church services. Pentecostal pastors must ensure that time and opportunity are given for the operation of spiritual gifts.

PREVENTING THE MISUSE OF SPIRITUAL GIFTS

It is also the pastor's solemn responsibility to see that the gifts of the Spirit are not misused in the services. When a few people are allowed to misuse spiritual gifts, the true moving of the Spirit is hindered. When the gifts are properly used the people are blessed and the church is strengthened.

Pastoral Supervision

Pastoring the spiritual gifts not only involves encouraging their use, it also involves monitoring their use to ensure that they are not misused or abused in the church. The gifts of the Spirit should bless the church and the community. However, when they are abused, they can become a curse rather than a blessing. Great harm is done to the church if the pastors allows an unbiblical use of spiritual gifts.

A church service must never become a disorderly gathering where every person is allowed to do "what seems right in his own eyes" (Judg. 21:25). Such church services cannot bring glory to Christ. Paul wrote that the gifts are to be ministered "in a fitting

Chapter 8: Pastoring the Spiritual Gifts

and orderly way" (1 Cor. 14:40). The pastor is responsible to ensure that scriptural order is maintained at all times.

Some carnal members may call their pastor "unspiritual" if he keeps proper order in the church. He should not fear such people. A true pastor is more interested in receiving God's approval than in avoiding man's criticism.

General Guidelines for Using the Gifts

In 1 Corinthians 12-14 the Bible gives us clear directions concerning spiritual gifts. Three general directions are as follows:

1. We should desire spiritual gifts (1 Cor. 12:31; 14:1, 39). We should desire these gifts because we have a big job to do. Spiritual gifts are the tools given by the Spirit that allow us to accomplish the work.

2. We should understand the purpose of the Spirit's gifts. Our definition of spiritual gifts states that their purpose is "to accomplish the will of the Father." Paul said that spiritual gifts were given "for the strengthening of the church" (1 Cor. 12:26). In the book of Acts we learn that the manifestation of spiritual gifts are also essential in advancing the kingdom of God among the lost. Thus, the purpose of the gifts is to bless the entire body of Christ and to reach the lost with the gospel. They must never be used to exalt or bring glory to an individual.

3. We must know how to use the gifts properly. The Corinthians believers knew about spiritual gifts (1 Cor. 12:1). In fact, they did "not lack any spiritual gift" (1 Cor. 1:7). However, they were ignorant about the proper use of those gifts. As a result, they were abusing spiritual gifts—especially the gift of tongues. We must understand and follow biblical guidelines for ministering spiritual gifts.

Specific Guidelines for the Prophetic Gifts

Pastoring the prophetic or vocal gifts (that is, prophecy, tongues, and the interpretation of tongues) in a local church is a special challenge. First Corinthians 14 tells how a church can maintain proper order in the use of these gifts. It gives us guidelines for the use of the prophetic gifts in congregational worship. Let's look at eleven of those guidelines:

Chapter 8: Pastoring the Spiritual Gifts

1. Tongues must be interpreted. The gift of tongues should always be interpreted (1 Cor. 14:5, 13, 16, 28).

2. Wait for interpretation. Once a message in tongues is given, the pastor should give time for an interpretation. He should encourage anyone who is feeling prompted by the Spirit to speak out in faith. The primary responsibility for interpreting the message falls upon the one who gave it (1 Cor. 14:13).

3. Maintain proper order. The gifts should be administered in proper order (1 Cor. 14:27). A pastor must never allow the service to get out of control. He must ensure that biblical order is maintained at all times.

4. Messages must be judged. Prophetic messages should always be judged by the congregation. The Bible says, "Two or three prophets speak, and the others should weigh carefully what is said" (1 Cor. 14:29). Pastors and other spiritual leaders are responsible to judge prophetic utterances in the body. A prophet who is not willing to have his or her words judged should not be allowed to speak in the church.

How can spiritual leaders judge if a message truly comes from God? The gift of discerning of spirits can be used here. This gift allows spiritual leaders to know what spirit is motivating the prophet. Those responsible for judging messages can also ask three questions: (1) Did the message agree with Scripture? (2) Was the message in harmony with the direction of the Spirit in the service? (3) Did the message build up and edify the congregation? The answer to each of these questions should be "yes." If the answer is to any of these questions is "no," the message must be judged to be out of order and must be corrected biblically.

5. Focus on edification. A message in tongues and interpretation should always edify or build up the body (1 Cor. 14:1–5, 12, 17). Paul said, "A tongue or an interpretation ... must be done for the strengthening of the body" (14:26). The pastor must ensure that the body is being edified by the prophetic gift. He must do this each time someone prophesies or gives a message in tongues with interpretation.

6. Use courtesy. The gifts should always be administered in Christian courtesy. Claiming to be "anointed" is no excuse for being rude or selfish. We should always consider other people's feelings. Paul said,

Chapter 8: Pastoring the Spiritual Gifts

If a revelation comes to someone who is sitting down, the first speaker should stop. For you can all prophesy in turn so that everyone may be instructed and encouraged. (1 Cor. 14:29–30)

7. Limit the number. Messages in tongues should be limited in number. Some church services seem to go on endlessly, with one message in tongues after another being given. The pastor must not allow this to happen. He must limit the number to two or three in any service (1 Cor. 14:27).

8. Control the gift. The one who prophesies can and should exercise control over his or her gift. Paul noted that "the spirits of the prophets are subject to the control of the prophets" (1 Cor. 14:27). No one can use the excuse, "I was 'in the Spirit' and could not control myself." A true prophet always has control over his own spirit.

9. Do not forbid tongues. Just because tongues should be controlled, does not mean that they should be forbidden in church (14:39). God wants the gift of tongues, as well as all of the gifts, to operate in the congregation. This assumes that the gift is manifested in proper order and edifies the church.

10. Exercised by those known to the church. Gifts should be manifested only through respected members of the local body or other trusted church leaders. The Bibles instructs us to "know them which labor among [us]" (1 Thess. 5:12, KJV). We should never allow a stranger or an impure person to exercise a spiritual gift in the congregation.

11. Properly respond. The pastor should lead the congregation in a proper response to a spiritual gift. Perhaps a prophetic message has just been given in the church. The pastor could lead the church in a time of individual or corporate response. He may feel led to call certain people forward for prayer. The pastor must use great care and wisdom in leading the congregational response.

Counseling the One Who Abuses Spiritual Gifts

If someone begins to abuse a spiritual gift, the pastor should first talk to that person in private. There, the pastor should give the person scriptural instructions concerning the proper use of these gifts. Hopefully, the person will be teachable and will listen to the pastor. Then the church will be blessed, and the person will grow spiritually.

However, the person may rebel against the pastor's advice and continue to abuse the gifts. If this happens, the pastor may have to publicly instruct (or even rebuke) him or her during a church service. It is usually wise to discuss such a case with other spiritual leaders before taking such action.

Some may ask, "Is it ever proper to stop someone from speaking in tongues in the congregation?" The answer is, "Yes, it is sometimes necessary to stop someone from speaking in tongues." This could happen (1) when the gift is clearly being abused, (2) when the speaker continues on and on, and the church is not being edified, and (3) when the speaker is causing disorder and confusion in the body (14:33).

CONCLUSION

The pastor is responsible for ensuring the free operation of spiritual gifts in the church. At the same time, he is responsible for preventing abuse of the gifts. He must, therefore, give constant supervision to the spiritual gifts. Pastoring the prophetic gifts—especially tongues—is a special challenge for a pastor. In some cases, those who abuse the gifts must be corrected. A pastor must, however, do everything in love. The goal is always that the gifts will be powerfully present and that the people are built up in the faith.

FOR REFLECTION AND REVIEW

1. What two skills must a Pentecostal pastor develop to ensure that the gifts are operating in the church?
2. What four topics should a pastor cover in teaching about spiritual gifts?
3. List four or more methods a pastor could use in teaching about spiritual gifts.
4. The pastor must model spiritual gifts for the congregation. What specific responsibility does this create for a pastor?
5. How can a pastor encourage his people to desire spiritual gifts?

Chapter 8: Pastoring the Spiritual Gifts

6. In what ways will both the church and the community be blessed as church members exercise spiritual gifts?
7. In what type of atmosphere do spiritual gifts operate best? How can a pastor develop such an atmosphere in his church?
8. What is a non-threatening atmosphere? How is this important to the operation of spiritual gifts in a local church?
9. State one reason why some pastors never see spiritual gifts operating in their services.
10. Why is pastoral supervision important to the operation of spiritual gifts?
11. Why is it important that the gifts not be abused in the congregation?
12. Summarize in your own words the instructions given in 1 Corinthians 14:40.
13. State three general guidelines that should govern our use of spiritual gifts.
14. What three questions can be asked when judging vocal gifts?
15. List eleven rules for the exercise of vocal gifts in the congregation.
16. What two things can a pastor do if someone is abusing the gifts of the Spirit?
18. When would it be proper to stop someone from speaking in tongues in the congregation?

Chapter 8: Pastoring the Spiritual Gifts

– Chapter 9 –

Divine Guidance
and
Power Encounter

If one is to be effective in power ministry, he or she must learn how to hear and properly respond to the voice of the Spirit. In this chapter we will address this important topic.

THE IMPORTANCE OF DIVINE GUIDANCE IN POWER MINISTRY

Important in the Ministry of Jesus

A careful study of the Gospel of John reveals that every act of Jesus' ministry was performed under the direct supervision of His Heavenly Father. Through the Spirit He was in constant communion with the Father, and always did as the Father directed. On one occasion He said,

> I tell you the truth, the Son can do nothing by himself; he can do only what he sees his Father doing, because whatever the Father does the Son also does. For the Father loves the Son and shows him all he does. (John 5:19-20, cf. John 8:28-29; 12:49)

Jesus did only what He "saw the Father doing." Every miracle He performed was orchestrated from heaven. He always and only did what His Heavenly Father told him to do.

There was once a man whom God had often used to heal the sick. Someone once challenged him, "If you have the gift of healing, why don't you go to the hospital and heal everyone there?" The man replied, "When Jesus went to the hospital He didn't heal everyone." "When did Jesus ever go to a hospital?" the first man asked. "He once went to Bethesda Hospital," the man said. "Read it for yourself in John 5:1-15. Although there were 'a great number of disabled people ... the blind, lame, and paralyzed' there, Jesus healed only one of them."

Sometimes Jesus would heal all who were sick in a given place (Matt. 4:23-24; 8:16). At other times he would heal only one, as at the Pool of Bethesda. So, why did Jesus heal only one man at Bethesda? In the verses following Jesus answered the question Himself: "The Son can do nothing by himself; he can do only what he sees his Father doing" (vv. 19-20). Jesus healed only one man at Bethesda because His Heavenly Father directed Him to heal only one man. As always, He did what he saw His Father doing.

This principle is an important key to any successful ministry, especially a ministry of power. We who desire to be used in such a ministry must learn from the example of Jesus. Just as Jesus' ministry in word and in deed was done under the Father's direct guidance, we too, if we are to minister in power and effectiveness, must perform our ministries under the direct guidance of the Heavenly Father. The only way for us to effectively minister in power is to hear and obey the voice of God. Like Jesus, we can only do what we see the Father doing—nothing more, nothing less.

If this is true, think how important it is that we be able to hear and know the voice of the Father. Without this ability little else in the way of effective ministry will follow.

Important in the Ministry of the Early Church
The apostles learned how to minister largely by observing and imitating the ministry of Jesus. Like Him, they constantly sought and received divine guidance in performing their ministries.

Jesus and the apostles often witnessed, in the words of John Wimber, by "divine appointment." In other words, God often set up the witnessing appointment for them, and then directed them into the witnessing situation. Here are three New Testament examples of individuals ministering by divine appointment:

1. Jesus and the Samaritan woman. In John 4:1-42 is found the fascinating story of a "revival" that occurred in the Samaritan town of Sychar. This revival began as a result of an act of personal

Chapter 9: Divine Guidance and Power Encounter

evangelism on the part of Jesus. He witnessed to, and won to Himself, a woman He met at the village well. But why did Jesus go to Samaria in the first place? He went there because His Heavenly Father sent Him there. In John 4:4 the Bible says, "Now he had to go through Samaria." Why was it so important for Him to go through Samaria? Because the Father had made a divine appointment for Him. There was a woman who needed Him, and a town ripe for revival.

2. Philip and the Ethiopian eunuch. The story of Philip and the Ethiopian eunuch is an example of one in the early church ministering by divine appointment (Acts 8:26-40). The Bible says, "Now the angel of the Lord said to Philip, 'Go south to the road—the desert road—that goes down from Jerusalem to Gaza'" (v. 26). God had set up an appointment for Philip with an African man who was hungry to know the living God. Upon finding the man riding in his chariot reading from Isaiah 53, the Spirit of the Lord spoke to Philip, "Go to that chariot and stay near it" (v. 30). As he drew near to the chariot, Philip heard the man reading aloud from the book. Philip began a conversation with the man that eventually led to the Ethiopian's conversion. Here again, we can see the importance of Philip's being able to hear the voice of the Spirit.

3. Peter and the household of Cornelius. A final example of ministering by divine appointment is found in Acts 10:1-48. In this story God Himself arranges a meeting between the Roman centurion, Cornelius, and Peter. Having set up the meeting, God then speaks to both Cornelius and Peter through visions (vv. 3-4, 10-11). He also spoke directly to Peter by His Spirit (v. 19). Read this wonderful story for yourself in your Bible.

In summary, if we, like Jesus and the apostles, are going to minister under divine guidance, we must learn how to hear and know the voice of God. This then brings us to the important question, How can one hear the voice of God? We will now seek to answer this important question.

HOW TO HEAR THE VOICE OF GOD

To be able to hear and recognize the voice of God we each need to understand and apply the following six principles:

Chapter 9: Divine Guidance and Power Encounter

Realize that God is Speaking to You

First, we must know that God does indeed speak to His children. In fact, He is likely speaking to each of us today! God is, by His very nature, a speaking God, and like any loving father, He speaks to His children on a regular basis. If you are not hearing the voice of God, it is not because He is not speaking to you, it is more likely because you do not know how to listen to Him.

Once a gardener was trying to water his garden. He was disturbed because no water was coming through his hose. He shouted angrily at the other gardener, "There is no water coming through this hose. I told you to turn the tap on!" The other gardener answered him, "Friend, the tap is turned on, but you have a kink in the hose at your end; so the water cannot come through." That is often how it is with us. God is speaking to us, but we are not hearing. We have a kink at our end of the hose.

Understand the Ways That God Speaks

Next, if we are going to be able to hear God's voice, we must understand the ways God speaks. Jesus said, "The sheep listen to [the Shepherd's] voice ... they know his voice" (John 10:3-4). God speaks to us today in four ways. We can call these the primary means, the dramatic means, the most usual means, and the confirmatory means. Let's briefly look at each means:

1. The Primary Means. God's primary means of speaking to man today is through His Word, the Holy Bible. If you want to know what God is saying to you, you can look in your Bible. This is the only absolutely reliable means we have of hearing the voice of God. Any other means must be weighed and judged by this primary means.

2. Dramatic Means. In addition, God sometimes speaks to his children through more dramatic means. In the Bible these dramatic means include dreams, visions, angelic visitations, and even God speaking in a audible voice. Of course, God can still do this today. However, a warning is in order. Sometimes certain unspiritual people, wanting to appear spiritual to others, claim that God has spoken to them by such dramatic means. As a result, many truly spiritual people shy away from such things as dreams and visions.

What, then, should our attitude be toward these things? First, we should realize that such dramatic means were not the most

Chapter 9: Divine Guidance and Power Encounter

common means God used to speak to His servants in the Bible. The most common means was by His Spirit to their spirit. (We will discuss this means next.) Nevertheless, while these dramatic means are not God's most common means of speaking to His children, they are obviously among the means He uses. The best stance we can take concerning these dramatic means is that we should not seek after such means; however, if God in His sovereignty chooses to speak to us through them, we should not doubt them.

3. The Most Usual Means. As mentioned above, God's most usual means of speaking to His children is by His Spirit to their spirits. Two Old Testaments passages serve as illustrations of this means. One is the example of the prophet Elijah. He did not hear God's voice in the dramatic means (that is, the great and powerful wind, the earthquake, or the fire), but he heard His voice as "a gentle whisper" (1 Kings 19:12-13). Another Old Testament example is the testimony of the prophet Isaiah. He described the voice of God like this: "Your ears will hear a voice behind you saying, 'This is the way; walk in it'" (Isa. 30:20).

The fact that God speaks to His servants Spirit to spirit is made even more clear in the New Testament. Paul said, "Those who are lead by the Spirit of God are the sons of God" (Rom. 8:14). He continues, "The Spirit Himself testifies with our spirit that we are God's children" (v. 16). Paul is saying that the Spirit of God speaks directly to the regenerated spirit of the born again Christian. This is the most common way we should expect God to speak to us today.

Paul expands on this theme in 1 Corinthians 2:9-13. Take a moment and carefully read and thoughtfully consider his words. In these verses Paul reveals three key concepts concerning how the Spirit of God speaks to our spirits. First, he confirms the fact that God reveals truth to us by His Spirit: "However, as it is written: 'No eye has seen, no ear has heard, no mind has conceived what God has prepared for those who love him'—*but God has revealed it to us by his Spirit.* The Spirit searches all things, even the deep things of God" (vv. 9-10, emphasis added)

Next, Paul compares the spirit in man with the Spirit of God. He says that a man's spirit inside of him knows his own thoughts. In the same way God's Spirit knows God's thoughts: "For who among men knows the thoughts of a man except the man's spirit within him? In the same way no one knows the thoughts of God except the Spirit of God" (v. 11).

Finally, Paul makes application of these two truths. He says that since God's Spirit knows God thoughts, and we have received God's Spirit, we can therefore know God's thoughts. His Spirit will reveal them to our spirits: "We have not received the spirit of the world but the Spirit who is from God, that we may understand what God has freely given us. This is what we speak, not in words taught us by human wisdom but in words taught by the Spirit..." (vv. 12-13, note also v. 16).

God's most common means of speaking to His children is by His Spirit to our spirits. As a child of God, you can expect to regularly hear God's voice speaking to you by this means.

4. Confirmatory Means. A final way we may hear the voice of God is through what has been called confirmatory means. Unlike the three direct means just mentioned above, confirmatory means are indirect means by which God speaks to us. In this way He uses circumstances or other people to speak to us. We mention three confirmatory means which God uses:

- *Providential circumstances.* One indirect confirmatory means God uses is providential circumstances. By this we mean those circumstances of life that God arranges to direct us and show us His will.
- *Spirit-filled believers.* Another confirmatory means that God uses to speak to us is through other Spirit-filled believers. In other words, God will speak His will to us through another believer. Sometimes this person will know that the message he is speaking is from God, at other times he will speak words that he does not really understand, but God will make them real to our own hearts.
- *Prophetic utterances.* Sometimes God will speak to us through prophetic utterances spoken in the context of a loving body of believers. These prophetic utterances include messages in tongues with interpretation and prophecies.

Again, we must offer a warning. Many of us have seen this means abused by immature and overzealous believers. Some have been lead astray and hurt by such false prophets. Remember two things when you feel that God may be speaking to you through others: First, what is spoken must be in total agreement with the Word of God. If it is not, you should immediately reject it as not coming from God. Next, what is spoken should only confirm what God has already spoken, or will speak, directly to your own spirit. Never let anyone tell you what God is saying to you without seriously weighing what is said. Always seek God for yourself until He has spoken directly to you by His Spirit to your spirit.

Prepare Your Heart to Hear God's Voice

One reason we fail to hear the voice of God when He speaks is because our hearts are not properly prepared to hear Him. Just as a radio receiver must be both plugged in and tuned in before it can receive the signal from the radio station, we too must be plugged in and tuned in to the Spirit before we can hear the voice of God.

We get "plugged in" when we are born again. It is through the new birth that our spirits are connected to the heavenly power Source, the Spirit of God. Paul said, "He who unites with the Lord is one with him in spirit" (1 Cor. 6:17). When we are born of the Spirit the Holy Spirit enters our being and we are made "new creations" in Christ (John 3:5; 2 Cor. 5:17). That is why Jesus said that once a man is born again he can "*see* the kingdom of God" (John 3:3). Further, Paul said, "The man without the Spirit ... cannot understand [the things that come from the Spirit of God], because they are spiritually discerned" (1 Cor. 2:14).

In addition to being born again, being plugged in to the power source involves being baptized in the Holy Spirit. It stands to reason that, if we are going to consistently and clearly hear the voice of the Spirit, we must be filled with the Spirit.[4] Being filled with the Spirit enhances one's ability to hear the voice of the Spirit. It could be compared to adding more power to our radio receiver, or to putting up a taller antenna. By being filled with they Spirit you will receive more power and more sensitivity to the voice of the Spirit.

---

[4]To find out how to be filled with the Spirit read Chapter 6.

Not only must we plug in to the Spirit of God, we must also "tune in" to His voice. Before a radio can receive a message from the radio station, it must also be tuned in to the proper channel. We tune in to God through the total commitment of ourselves to God and to His perfect will for our lives. The Bible warns us, "So, as the Holy Spirit says: Today, if you will hear his voice, do not harden your hearts" (Heb. 3:6-7). We need to keep our hearts open and tender before Him. Such a sensitivity to the Spirit of God can arise only from a humble and obedient spirit. It can come only through a consistent devotional life, including much time spent in prayer and meditation on the Word.

Learn How to Recognize God's Voice
Further, if we are to consistently and clearly hear the voice of God, we must learn to recognize His voice when He speaks. Jesus said, "The sheep listen to [the Shepherd's] voice ... they know his voice" (John 10:3-4). Such an ability to know the Shepherd's voice comes only through practice (Heb. 5:14). As we practice hearing and obeying the voice of the Spirit, we learn to more clearly recognize His voice when He speaks.

Test the "Voice" to Prove if It is Truly God's
It is also essential that we learn to test the voices that we "hear" in order to determine whether they are truly the voice of God. The Bible tells us that there are "many kinds of voices in the world" (1 Cor. 14:10, KJV). These voices include human voices—both our own inner voice (our personal thoughts), and outer voices (other people). These voices also include spiritual voices, including thoughts that can be planted in our minds by God, or even by evil spirits. It is essential that we know how to test these voices to know whether or not they come from God. If they are not in total agreement with the Word of God they should be rejected.

By Faith, Practice Obeying the Voice of God
A final principle we must understand is this: if we are to learn to recognize the voice of God, we must, by faith, begin obeying His voice when we do hear it. We really have but one good reason to hear God's voice: we hear His voice in order that we might obey

Chapter 9: Divine Guidance and Power Encounter

it. What then should we do? We should expect God to speak, and when He does speak, we must obey. As we obey and follow, we learn to better discern the voice of God.

The ability to know and the faith to obey the voice of God are essential requirements for power ministry. We should make it our aim to learn how to do both.

FOR REFLECTION AND REVIEW

1. Explain how Jesus sought His Father's guidance in His ministry.
2. What do we mean when we say that the apostles often witnessed by "divine appointment?"
3. Describe how Jesus was divinely guided to witness to the Samaritan woman?
4. Did Philip just happen upon the Ethiopian eunuch on the desert road? Explain your answer.
5. Describe how the Holy Spirit set up the meeting between Peter and Cornelius' household.
6. Does God speak to us today? Then why are we not hearing His voice?
7. What is the primary means by which God speaks today?
8. What do we mean when we say God speaks by "more dramatic means?" What are some of these means?
9. What is the best stance we can take concerning these more dramatic means whereby God speaks to us?
10. What is the most usual means that God uses to speak to His children?
11. Cite two Old Testament texts and three New Testament texts that show us this means by which God speaks.
12. List three "confirmatory means" that God uses.
13. What two things should we always remember when we feel that God is speaking to us through another person?
14. List four means whereby God speaks to us today.
15. What do we mean when we say we must be "plugged in" before we can hear the voice of God?
16. What do we mean when we say we must be "tuned in" before we can hear the voice of God?
17. Name two ways we can learn to better hear the voice of God.

Chapter 9: Divine Guidance and Power Encounter

18. State one way we can test to see if the "voice" we hear is truly God's voice.
19. State one way we can learn to better discern the voice of God.

Chapter 10

The Weapons of Our Warfare

In Chapter 3 we learned that Christ came to establish God's kingdom in this world. He will do this through His church, anointed by the Holy Spirit. Because Satan is opposing the advancement of God's kingdom, a great spiritual war has broken out. Now, whether we like it or not— whether we even know it or not!—the church is involved in a great war with the kingdom of Satan (Eph. 6:12). In this war Christ has given to us power and authority over our enemy. Jesus once told His disciples,

> I saw Satan fall like lighting from heaven. I have given you authority to trample on snakes and scorpions and to overcome all the power of the enemy; nothing will harm you. (Luke 10:19-20)

For any war to be fought successfully requires weapons. Likewise, our spiritual warfare requires spiritual weapons. As the army of Christ we have been equipped with all the necessary spiritual weapons we need to defeat Satan. Paul spoke of these mighty spiritual weapons: "The weapons we fight with are not the weapons of the world. On the contrary, they have divine power to demolish strongholds" (2 Cor. 10:4).

In this chapter we will seek to identify these spiritual weapons and discuss how each may be used to fight and win spiritual battles against Satan and his demonic minions.

Chapter 10: The Weapons of Our Warfare

ALL THE WEAPONS IN GOD'S ARMORY

In Ephesians 6:10-18 we are told to put on the full armor of God, or as Ronald Knox translates this passage, "You are to wear all the weapons in God's armory"[1] We are told to take up God's weapons so we can take our stand against the devil. What, then, are these weapons in God's armory, and how can we use it to defeat the devil?

Our Source of Strength for Battle

We must remember that the source of our strength for the battle is not human but divine. The Bible tells us to "be strong in the Lord and in his mighty power" (v. 10). We are not to look to our own strength, nor our own resources, to fight this spiritual battle. We are to look to God for His strength and His resources.

And yet, while we don't look to our own strength, there is something that we must do: We must "put on the full armor of God so that [we] can take [our] stand against the devil's schemes" (v. 11).

The Purposes of the Whole Armor of God

Paul tells us the purposes for this spiritual armor. They are two: First, that we might stand our ground against the enemy's attacks (v. 13), and second, that we might not fall prey to Satan's "schemes" (v. 11). The word translated "schemes" in verse 11 comes from the Greek word, *methodeia*. It is translated into English in various ways, including "methods," "strategies," "cunning," "wiles," "devices," and "stratagems." We are, therefore, to be prepared for both the enemy's attacks and the enemy's strategies.

The Specifics of the Whole Armor of God

Paul used the arming of a Roman legionnaire as a means of illustrating the various items in the Christian's spiritual arsenal, as follows:

---

[1] *The New Testament in the Translation of Monsignor Ronald Knox* (Sheed and Ward, 1944).

Chapter 10: The Weapons of Our Warfare

Stand firm then, with the belt of *truth* buckled around your waist, with the breastplate of *righteousness* in place, and with your feet fitted with the *readiness* that comes from the gospel of peace. In addition to all this, take up the shield of *faith*, with which you can extinguish all the flaming arrows of the evil one. Take the helmet of *salvation* and the sword of the Spirit, which is the *word of God.* And *pray in the Spirit* on all occasions with all kinds of prayers and requests. With this in mind, be alert and always keep on praying for all the saints. (Eph. 4:14-18, emphases added).

You will notice that we emphasized seven key words and phrases in the above passage. Each word or phrase speaks of a powerful weapon in the Christian's arsenal. There are thus seven ways that we can arm ourselves to do spiritual battle with the devil:

1. Armed with Truth. We, as Christian warriors, are to be armed with truth. To put on the belt of truth could mean two things: First it could mean that we are to be armed with the Word of God, which is truth (John 17:17). We should fill our hearts and minds with the words of the Bible. It could also mean that we are to arm ourselves with truthfulness, that is, with absolute honesty and integrity.

We are to arm ourselves in order that we may stand against the attacks and schemes of Satan. Think with me for a moment. Against what scheme of Satan can the weapon of truth be used? It can be used against Satan's lies. The lie is one of the devil's most powerful weapons. Remember, he is the father of all liars (John 8:44). We can stand against his lies by proclaiming the truth of God's word and by living lives of honesty and integrity before God and men.

2. Armed with Righteousness. In our battles with Satan we are also to be armed with righteousness. Righteousness can be defined both as right relationship and as right living. We can be truly righteous only if we are in right relationship with God through Jesus Christ. As a result of this relationship we are to practice right living; that is, we are to live clean and holy lives. We must know how to "say 'No' to ungodliness and worldly passions, and to live self-controlled, and upright and godly lives in this present age" (Titus 2:12). Thus, by putting on righteousness, we will be able to

Chapter 10: The Weapons of Our Warfare

withstand Satan's tentacles of wickedness that have defeated so many.

3. Armed with Readiness. Next, Paul tells that we are to be armed with readiness. In other words, we are to be vigilant and constantly alert for the attacks of the enemy. Peter warned us, "Be self-controlled and alert. Your enemy the devil prowls around like a roaring lion looking for someone to devour" (1 Pet. 5:8). We must be well equipped and prepared for any cunning and treacherous attack of the enemy.

Note how Paul says that this alertness is produced by the gospel (v. 15). It is the proclamation of the gospel that alerts, prepares, and equips men concerning the enemies tactics.[2]

4. Armed with Faith. Another weapon we are to take up in our battle against Satan is the weapon of faith. The faith we are to take up must surely include saving faith, that is, a basic trust in God and in His provision of salvation through the atoning work of Christ on the cross. This weapon of faith, however, must go beyond saving faith. It must also include a more active kind of faith that aggressively reaches out an takes what God has promised. Such faith can be used as a shield to "extinguish all the flaming arrows of the evil one" (Eph. 6:16). With this weapon we can counter every enemy attack. These attacks can include unsought and unholy thoughts, desires to disobey, rebellious suggestions, lust, and fear.

Not only is faith a trustworthy defensive weapon, as mentioned above, it is also a powerful offensive weapon that can be used to defeat the enemy. Take time now to read Hebrews 11. In this great "faith chapter" you will see how men and women of old used faith as a powerful offensive weapon. Through faith they "conquered kingdoms, administered justice, and gained what was promised" (v. 33). Through faith they "became powerful in battle and routed foreign armies" (v. 34). In fact, the entire Bible is full of such men and women who used faith as a mighty weapon to advance the

---

[2]For a more detailed discussion of the power of the gospel see Chapter 4, "Power Ministry and Preaching the Gospel."

Chapter 10: The Weapons of Our Warfare

kingdom of God in the earth. We, too, must learn to use this powerful spiritual weapon.

5. Armed with Salvation. A fifth weapon in the Christian's arsenal against the devil is the weapon of salvation. Here, we should interpret salvation in the broadest sense. We are speaking not only of salvation from sin and hell, but also of any salvation, or deliverance, that comes from God. This could include salvation from demons, danger, sickness, and death. It also includes deliverance from Satan and his hidden traps and snares.

This salvation can only come from God. To receive it, all we have to do is to call on the name of the Lord (Rom. 10:13). When snared by the enemy and taken "prisoner of war," we must remember that all is not lost. We can call on our mighty Deliverer, and He will save us!

6. Armed with the Word of God. One of our most powerful spiritual weapons is the Word of God, described in our text as the "sword of the Spirit." There are two possible applications of this exhortation for the Christian worker to "take ... the word of God." First, it means we are to be armed with the Bible. To arm ourselves with the Bible we must read, know, memorize, study, apply, and preach the Word of God.

The word of God in this passage could also be referring to a specific, personal "word" that we might receive from God. This word could be a specific passage of Scripture that the Lord speaks to your heart in order to meet a specific need. It could also be a specific revelation from God to meet a special need, including words of knowledge and wisdom.

Whether it is the whole counsel of God (the entire Bible), or a specific verse of Scripture, this weapon can be used for both offensive and a defensive battle. It can be used as an offensive weapon when it is preached and taught under an anointing of the Spirit. It can be used as a defensive weapon to counter Satan's attacks. When Satan comes against us with His lies, we can hurl the promises of God's Word in His face, just as did Jesus in the wilderness (Luke 4:1-12). Satan must retreat against such an attack! (v. 13).

7. Armed with Prayer in the Spirit. A final spiritual weapon mentioned in this passage "prayer in the Spirit" (v. 18). Prayer in the Spirit is any kind of Spirit-anointed, Spirit-directed prayer. It is also, I believe, speaking more specifically of prayer in tongues (compare 1 Cor. 14:14 with Rom. 6:26). Praying in the Spirit is a powerful spiritual weapon in the hands of the Spirit-filled saint. Paul says that we should never put this weapon down; we should "pray in the Spirit on all occasions" (v. 18). As the spiritual warrior prays in the Spirit, many blessings follow: his mind is renewed, his spiritual life is strengthened (1 Cor. 14:4), his faith is built up (Jude 20), and his prayer is according to the will of God (Rom. 8:27).

SEVEN ADDITIONAL POWERFUL SPIRITUAL WEAPONS

In addition to what we have just mentioned, there are seven other powerful spiritual weapons at the believer's disposal. Some, because they are discussed at some length elsewhere in this book, will be only mentioned briefly. It is good, however, to group them together in this chapter. This will help the reader to see how many weapons he or she has at their disposal in their battle against the devil.

The Weapon of Fasting

One powerful spiritual weapon is the weapon of fasting. Fasting is to be used with the weapon of prayer. In the story of the demon possessed boy (Mark 9:14-29) Jesus' disciples try unsuccessfully to cast a demon out of the boy. Later, when Jesus' disciples ask Him, "Why could we not cast him out?" Jesus answered them, "*This kind* can come out by nothing but prayer and fasting" (Mark 9:29 [NKJV], emphasis added). *This kind* of demon still exists! Prayer with fasting is often the only means to victory over such evil spirits. A veteran missionary to Africa once told me that whenever he was unsuccessful in casting a demon out of a person, he would always enter into a time of prayer and fasting before trying again. Every time he used this tactic the demon was successfully exorcized.

The Scriptures speak of at least four ways we can use the spiritual weapon of fasting: to help gain audience with God (Ezra 8:23), to set the captives free (Isa. 58:6), to gain wisdom and understanding (Dan. 9:2, 3, 21-22), and to find the will of God in a given matter (Acts 13:2). Take time to look up and meditate on each of these references. This exercise will help you to understand how powerful the weapon of fasting is.

The Weapon of Praise

Another powerful weapon is the weapon of praise. Although praise is not often thought of as a spiritual weapon, there is great spiritual power generated in Spirit-inspired praise. When the children of Israel shouted, the walls of a Jericho fell (Josh. 6:16-20). When the singers of Jehoshaphat began to praise the beauty of God's holiness, God came on the scene and set ambushes against the armies of Ammon, Moab, and Mount Seir (2 Chron. 20:1-26). As Paul and Silas prayed and sang hymns to God at midnight in a Roman prison, the power of God was manifested: "Suddenly there was such a violent earthquake that the foundations of the prison were shaken. At once all the prison doors flew open, and everybody's chains came loose" (Acts 16:26).

As we praise God, His presence and power enter into our situation (Psa. 22:3 [NKJV]), and our enemy is confused and routed. Praise is a mighty weapon at the believer's disposal.

The Weapon of Love

Love is another of our spiritual weapons. Genuine love has amazing power in directing men and women to Christ. Some, who cannot be persuaded by our logical arguments, or even our manifestations of power, can be won to Christ through a simple demonstration of Christian love. Saul of Tarsus was, in part, persuaded to turn to Christ because of the powerful demonstration of love he witnessed in Stephen. As the stones beat out Stephen's life, he prayed, "Lord, do not hold this sin against them" (Acts 7:60). This demonstration of love had a great impact on Saul's mind, and prepared him for his eventual encounter with the risen Christ on the Damascus Road. Paul tells us one way we may use this weapon of love:

> Do not repay anyone evil for evil. Be careful to do what is right in the eyes of everybody... "If your enemy is hungry, feed him; if he is thirsty, give him something to drink. In doing this, you will heap burning coals on his head." Do not be overcome by evil, but overcome evil with good. (Rom. 12:17, 20-21)

Chapter 10: The Weapons of Our Warfare

Thus, evil can be overcome by good, and men and women won to Christ with the powerful weapon of love.

The Weapon of the Holy Spirit

In Acts 1:8 Jesus said that His followers would receive power after the Holy Spirit came upon them. He was speaking about the experience of the baptism in the Holy Spirit (Acts 1:4). This clothing of power from on high is an indispensable weapon for spiritual warfare.[3]

The Weapons of the Gifts of the Spirit

One primary reason spiritual gifts were given to the church is to do spiritual warfare. Through these gifts the army of God is able to receive orders and directions from its Commander-in-Chief (revelation gifts); to speak powerful words from heaven (prophetic gifts); and to release the power of God against the enemy (power gifts).[4]

The Weapon of Jesus' Name

Jesus has also given us His name as a spiritual weapon to be used against the forces of evil. All the authority of heaven stands behind the name of Jesus. When we use His name as He has directed, we speak with the authority of heaven. The powers of hell must yield to that Name that is above every name (Phil. 2:9-11). Jesus taught us to pray in His name:

> I tell you the truth, anyone who has faith in me will do what I have been doing. He will do even greater things than these, because I am going to the Father. And I will do whatever you ask in my name, so that the Son may bring glory to the Father. You

---

[3]For a detailed explanation of this divine gift see Chapter 6, "The Baptism in the Holy Spirit and Power Ministry."

[4]For a discussion of the nature and use of spiritual gifts see Chapter 7, "The Gifts of the Holy Spirit and Power Ministry."

Chapter 10: The Weapons of Our Warfare

may ask me for anything in my name, and I will do it. (John 14:12-14)

In that day you will no longer ask me anything. I tell you the truth, my Father will give you whatever you ask in my name. Until now you have not asked for anything in my name. Ask and you will receive, and your joy will be complete. (John 16:23-24)

The apostles often used the name of Jesus to heal the sick, cast out demons, and to do the works of Jesus (Acts 3:6). We, too, can use this powerful spiritual weapon to accomplish the same things.

The Weapon of the Gospel
The gospel, that is, the message of Christ, is a mighty spiritual weapon. Paul called it "the power of God for the salvation of everyone who believes" (Rom. 1:16). He said that it has the power to create faith in the hearts of those who hear it preached (Rom. 10:17). As the gospel is preached the power of God is released. What a powerful weapon is the proclamation of Christ![5]

God has given us many powerful spiritual weapons that we may use to confront and defeat the powers of Satan. As His spiritual warriors, we must set ourselves to learn how to effectively wield each one.

FOR REFLECTION AND REVIEW

1. Describe the kind of war the church is involved in.
2. What kind of weapons must we use to fight this war? Why?
3. To whom do we look as our source of strength for the battle? What must we do ourselves?
4. What are the two purposes for our spiritual armor?
5. To be armed with truth could mean two things. What are they?
6. What scheme of the devil can we combat with the weapon of truth?
7. In what two ways can we be armed with righteousness?

---

[5]For a thorough treatment of this subject see Chapter 4, "Power Ministry and Preaching the Gospel."

Chapter 10: The Weapons of Our Warfare

8. What snare of the devil may we avoid by being armed with righteousness?
9. What does it mean to be armed with readiness? What produces this readiness in us? How is this readiness produced?
10. When we speak of the weapon of faith, what kind of faith do we speak of?
11. In speaking of the weapon of salvation, what do we mean when we say that we should interpret the word "salvation" in the broadest sense?
12. Name two ways we can take up the word of God as a weapon against Satan.
13. What two ways can we define prayer in the Spirit?
14. List the seven spiritual weapons spoken of in Ephesians 6:14-18.
15. Name four benefits of using the weapon of fasting.
16. THINK: Jesus spoke of "this kind" of demon. Does this mean that there are various kinds of demons? Give reasons for your answer.
17. State three biblical examples where the people of God won victories by using the weapon of praise.
18. How can we use the weapon of love to fight spiritual battles?
19. According to Acts 1:8 what happens to a Christian when he or she is filled with the Holy Spirit?
20. State one important reason why Christ has given spiritual gifts to His church.
21. When we use the name of Jesus as God directs us, what does God do? What must demons and illnesses do?
22. What special power does the gospel have?
23. List the seven additional spiritual weapons discussed in this section.

– Part III –

The "How To"
of a
Power Ministry

– Chapter 11 –

How To Heal the Sick

We now begin the third and final part of our study, entitled "The 'How To' of a Power Ministry." The purpose of this section is to help us know how to put into actual practice the principles we have studied in the previous chapters. In our first lesson of this section we will deal with how to heal the sick; in the second we will consider how to cast out demons; in the third we will discuss how to lead people into the vital experience of the baptism in the Holy Spirit, and in the final lesson we will deal with the role of power ministry in campaign evangelism. Learn these lessons well. You can then go out and begin to apply the things you have learned.

This lesson presents a practical "how to" model for healing the sick. The model we will suggest is both scriptural and pastoral. It is *scriptural* because it is based on the practice of Jesus and the apostles. It is *pastoral* because we will approach the subject from the perspective of a local church pastor. Unlike the campaign evangelist, the pastor is often involved in praying, not for nameless masses of people, but for one person at a time. And the person for whom he or she is praying is a person they know, love, and associate with on a regular basis.

True pastors are deeply concerned with the personal feelings and needs of the ones to whom they minister. Their goal is that, whatever the results of their prayers, the people to whom they ministering will feel more loved by God, and more loved by the church, than before the ministry engagement. The true pastor will never run roughshod over the individual, condemning or accusing him of not having faith, but he, like Jesus, always minister in loving concern for the feelings of the person.

PRELIMINARY CONSIDERATIONS

Before we discuss the particulars of how to heal the sick, let's turn our attention to some preliminary considerations:

The Healing Environment

The healing environment is the spiritual atmosphere surrounding a ministry encounter. The ministry encounter could include healing the sick, casting out demons, or any other ministry requiring a demonstration of the Spirit's power. When a minister approaches such a ministry encounter, it is essential that he or she give careful consideration to the environment.

Luke spoke of such an environment that attended the healing ministry of Jesus: "Great crowds of people came to hear him and to be healed of their sicknesses… And the power of the Lord was present for him to heal the sick" (Luke 5:15, 17). Notice how Jesus ministered healing in an atmosphere filled with the divine Presence: "the power of the Lord was present."

On one occasion, when He was about to raise Jairus' daughter from the dead, Jesus addressed the spiritual atmosphere surrounding this ministry encounter:

> When they came to the home of the synagogue ruler, Jesus saw a commotion, with people crying and wailing loudly, He went in and said to them, "Why all this commotion and wailing? The child is not dead but asleep." But they laughed at him. After he put them all out, he took the child's father and mother and the disciples who were with him, and went in where the child was. He took her by the hand and said to her, "Talitha Koum!"… Immediately the girl stood up and walked around. (Mark 5:39-42)

Notice how, before Jesus performed the miracle, He first put those who were unbelieving and hostile to His ministry out of the room. He was clearly managing the spiritual environment. Peter did much the same thing when he raised Dorcas from the dead (Acts 9:40).

On one occasion Jesus was hindered in His healing ministry because of an atmosphere of unbelief. The Bible says that in His home town of Nazareth "He could not do any miracles ... except lay his hands on a few sick people and heal them. And he was amazed at their lack of faith" (Mark 6:5-6, ref. Matt.13:58). These incidents reveal two important characteristics that mark a healing environment:

1. The Manifest Presence of God. First, a healing environment is marked by the manifest presence of God. As mentioned earlier in this book, the manifest presence of God is the felt or perceptible presence of God. Luke spoke of such a presence that attended the ministry of Jesus: "And the power of the Lord was present to heal the sick" (Luke 5:17).[6]

2. Expectant Faith. A healing environment is also characterized by an expectant faith on the part of those present. Expectant faith is the faith that is present when people anticipate a miracle from God. It is the kind of faith exhibited by the sick woman who said, "If I just touch his clothes, I will be healed" (Mark 5:28). A wise minister can, through a clear presentation of the gospel, which includes strong emphases on faith and healing, help to inspire such expectant faith in the hearts of the people.

Personal Preparation of the Minister

Although we have already spoken in general terms about preparation for power ministry,[7] we feel it is necessary to speak here about the minister's immediate preparation for a healing

---

[6] Other examples of the manifest presence of God can be found in the following scriptures: Exod.3:1-6; 2 Chron. 7:1-3; Luke 2:8-9; Acts 2:1-13; 4:31; and 1 Cor.14:22-25.

[7] See Chapter 5, "Essential Elements and Preparation for a Power Ministry."

encounter. There are six actions one can take to prepare himself or herself for a healing encounter:

1. Ask for a fresh infilling of the Holy Spirit. Continue in prayer until you sense the Spirit's presence.
2. Seek to remind yourself of who Jesus is, what He has done, and what He has told you to do. Don't forget, it is only through Jesus, and faith in Him, that the victory will come.
3. Seek to empty yourself of "self." Remember, by yourself you can do nothing (John 15:5).
4. Try to empty your mind of all preconceptions and presuppositions concerning how the healing or deliverance will take place. In Scripture no two cases of healing were identical in the ministry required.
5. Ask God, "What do You want to do?" (John 5:19-20). Once you discover God's will in the matter, submit yourself absolutely to that will. You can now proceed in boldness and faith.
6. Frequently pray in the Spirit, constantly listening for the Spirit's voice to direct you.

How the Anointing for Ministry Comes

In Chapter 7 we said that spiritual gifts, including the power gifts, come as "anointings" of the Holy Spirit. How, then, do these anointings come upon an individual for ministry? Some testify of an inner surge or a sudden infusion of power, "heat," or "tingling." Others say that these anointings come with a feeling of deep compassion for the one being ministered to, or a full assurance that the work will be done. In the gospels we often see Jesus "filled with compassion" before healing the sick (Mark 1:41). (More on this later.) Still others testify that along with these inner promptings there may come a "knowing" that God wants the healing done, or a sudden confident faith that God will heal or work a miracle. However the anointing comes to you personally, you will sense in your spirit that the Spirit of God is working in the situation.

HOW TO HEAL THE SICK: A THREE-STEP PASTORAL MODEL

I will suggest a three-step pastoral model for healing the sick. This model is a common sense approach based on the healing ministry of Jesus and the apostles. It seeks to answer three important questions about the healing encounter: "What is the person's real need? How will the minister proceed with ministry? How will he or she advise this person after the ministry engagement?"

Step 1: the Interview

Step one in the healing encounter is to discover what the individual's real need is. Too many times we immediately begin to pray for a person, not even knowing what we should pray for. This is both foolish and tragic, because we often pray for the wrong thing. And, just as often, the person leaves without his or her need being met. Therefore, we must begin the healing encounter by asking a few questions.

A good beginning question is, "What would you like God to do for you today?" Once we have asked the question, we then listen very closely to what the person has to say. We "listen" four ways: with our *ears,* with our *eyes,* with our *heart,* and with our *spirit.* With our ears we listen closely to what the person is saying; with our eyes we watch to see what God is already doing, and how the individual is responding to the Spirit of God; with our heart we feel his pain and sense his faith; and with our spirit we listen closely to what the Spirit is whispering to us.

Before proceeding with ministry we must make two important decisions: First, we must make a "diagnostic decision," that is, we must decide what the problem is. Next, we must make a "ministry decision," that is, we must decide how we will proceed in ministry.

In the *diagnostic decision* we seek to determine what is wrong with the individual and what is the cause of his or her problem. Before we begin the healing encounter we need to know where the person is hurting and why he has this condition. Is the source of the illness natural, or is it demonic? The answers to these questions will help to determine how we proceed in ministry.

Next, we must make a *ministry decision.* Here we decide how to proceed in ministry. We must ask, "Do I need to cast out a demon, or do I need to pray a prayer of faith? If I am to proceed with a healing encounter, what scriptural method(s) should I use?" All along it is essential that we remain sensitive to the voice and leading of the Holy Spirit.

Step 2: Ministry Engagement

The next step in the healing encounter we call the *ministry engagement.* We now act based on our diagnostic and ministry decisions. We may proceed by asking the Holy Spirit to come and manifest His power. We can minister healing through the laying on of hands, words of faith, commands of faith, declarations, petitions, teaching, the release of power, the prayer of agreement, binding and loosing, or some other biblical method. (We will discuss these methods later in this chapter.)

It is important to remember that, as we proceed with ministry, we should remain sensitive to what God is doing. Watch for indications of the Spirit's work. Ask yourself, "What is God doing right now in this situation?" You may ask the individual, "What are you feeling?" "Has the pain gone away?" "Do you sense that anything is happening?" As you discover what God is doing for the individual, continue to minister, following the Spirit's leading.

It is important that we not stop too soon in the healing engagement. Sometimes the healing is a process and takes time (for example, Mark 8:22-25). Continue to pray until the person is healed or you sense a release from the Spirit to stop.

Step 3: Post-prayer Guidance

Our ministry is not finished until we have given post-prayer guidance to the person we have just prayed for. Jesus Himself often gave post-prayer guidance (for example, Mark 5:19; John 5:14; 9:35-39). If the person has received healing, encourage him to continue in faith and obedience. If he is only partially healed—and this is often the case—encourage him to trust God for the completion of the healing. If he doesn't receive healing, assure him of God's continuing love and Christ's healing power. Let him know that you will continue to pray and believe God with him for his healing. You may want to ask him to return for another prayer session.

HOW JESUS HEALED THE SICK

How did Jesus heal the sick? This is an important question since He is our example for ministry. As we observe the healing ministry of Jesus we can see a pattern for our own healing ministries.

Concerning the healing ministry of Jesus, Jim Miller has noted, "One important observation will reveal itself as you study Christ's methods in healing the sick: He never healed the sick twice in the same way. However, it is also important to observe that He limited the number of methods He used to no more than ten in an unlimited variety of combinations."[8] In his two insightful charts, "The Healing Ministry of Jesus" and "The Healing Methods of Christ" Miller outlines in detail the healing ministry of Christ (Appendices 1 and 2). Let's now look at some of the healing methods Jesus:

Speaking a Word

Jesus' most common method of healing the sick was by speaking a word to the one being healed:

- Sometimes this was a command to the sick person to do something:
  - "Pick up your mat and walk" (John 5:8).
  - "Stretch out your hand" (Mark 3:5).
  - "Young man, I say unto you get up" (Luke 7:14).
- At other times it was a command for demons to leave:
  - "Be quiet ... Come out of him!" (Mark 1:25).
  - "Come out of this man, you evil spirit!" (Mark 5:8).
  - "You deaf and mute spirit ... I command you, come out of him and never enter him again" (Mark 9:25).
- Sometimes He spoke directly to the illness or condition:
  - "Be clean!" (Matt. 8:3; Mark 8:41).

---

[8] Jim Miller, "How to Heal the Sick, an Overview" (an unpublished monograph), 3.

Chapter 11: How to Heal the Sick

- "Receive your sight" (Luke 18:42).
- "Be opened!" (Mark 7:34).
* Sometimes His word was an acknowledgment of the faith of the recipient:
  - "Your faith has healed you" (Matt. 8:22).
* Or a simple statement of the fact that the healing had taken place:
  - "Woman you are set free from your infirmity" (Luke.13:12).
  - "Your son will live" (John 5:50).

Touching or Laying on of Hands

Another common healing method of Jesus was touching or laying hands on the sick person:

* "He touched her hand and the fever left her" (Matt. 8:15).
* "Jesus ... touched their eyes, and immediately they received their sight..." (Matt. 20:34).
* "Jesus put his fingers into the man's ears ... and touched the man's tongue. At this, the man's ears were opened, his tongue was loosened..." (Mark 7:33-35).
* "Laying hands on each one, he healed them" (Luke 4:40).

Faith

On some occasions Jesus responded to and acknowledged faith as the prime ingredient effecting healing:

* Sometimes He noted the faith of the recipient of healing:
  - "Go ... your faith has healed you." (Matt. 10:52).
  - "Woman, you have great faith! Your request is granted" (Matt. 15:28).
* On other occasions He acknowledged the faith of others:
  - "Jesus saw their [the friends of the paralytic] faith..." (Mark 2:5).

Compassion

As briefly noted above, the gospels sometime specifically mention His compassion as a prime ingredient in healing the sick:

Chapter 11: How to Heal the Sick

- "He had compassion on them and healed them (Matt. 14:14).
- "Filled with compassion Jesus reached out his hand and touched the man..." (Mark 1:41-42).
- "When the Lord saw her, his heart went out to her... Then he ... touched the coffin... The dead man set up, and began to talk" (Luke 7:13-15).

Release of Power

The Bible indicates that Jesus did His works in the power and anointing of the Holy Spirit (Acts 10:38; Luke 4:17-18; 5:17). Many of his miracles resulted from a release of power that flowed from Him into the recipients' bodies, resulting in their healing:

- "Power was coming from him and healing them all" (Luke 6:19).
- "Someone touched me; I know that power has gone out from me" (Luke 8:46).

The Name of Jesus

A careful examination of the healings performed by the disciples in the book of Acts shows that they often imitated and duplicated the methods of Jesus; however, there was one important addition. They did it in the name of Jesus (Mark 16:17-18; Acts 4:10). Today, we, too, should seek to imitate the methods of Jesus with this one essential addition—we must do it in the powerful Name of Jesus!

We, as ministers of Christ, have been given a clear commission from Him. We are to preach the gospel, and we are to heal the sick. Jesus has given us a clear model of how we must do this. Our job is to move out in simple faith and obedience, imitating His methods and expecting Him to confirm His Word with signs following.

FOR REFLECTION AND REVIEW

1. What do we mean when we say that the model we will use for healing the sick is scriptural?

Chapter 11: How to Heal the Sick

2. What do we mean when we say it is pastoral?
3. Define the term "healing environment."
4. What two characteristics mark a healing environment?
5. What six things can the minister do to prepare for a healing encounter?
6. What is a good question to ask when beginning a healing encounter?
7. List and explain four ways the minister should "listen" during the interview step.
8. What is meant by the term "diagnostic decision?"
9. What is meant by the term "ministry decision?"
10. List the actions a minister can take in healing the sick during the ministry engagement.
11. Why should the healing minister not stop too soon in a healing engagement?
12. Define the term "post-prayer guidance."
13. What counsel should be given if the person receives healing? If the person is only partially healed? If the person is not healed?
14. Why is it important that we study how Jesus healed the sick?
15. What was Jesus' most common way of healing the sick? What five forms did this method take?
16. Cite four examples of Jesus healing the sick by touching or the laying on of hands.
17. Cite three examples of Jesus acknowledging or responding to faith, noting whose faith He responded to in each case.
18. List three examples where compassion for the suffering was a key ingredient in Jesus' healing method.
21. Cite two examples of Jesus healing the sick though a release of power.
20. In imitating the healing methods of Jesus, what important addition did the apostles make?

– Chapter 12 –

How to Cast Out Demons

As the church goes into the world with the gospel, one of its first orders of business is to confront and conquer the powers of darkness in the name of Jesus. It is interesting to note that Jesus' first miracle recorded in Mark's gospel involved the casting out of demons (Mark 1:21-27), and the first sign to follow believers spoken of in the Mark's version of the Great Commission is "In my name they will drive out demons…" (Mark 16:17).

In Chapter 3 we discussed how the coming of God's kingdom into the world results in conflict with Satan and his demonic forces. These evil legions will stubbornly resist the coming of Christ's kingdom, whether it be into a geographical locality or into the life of an individual. Demons must therefore be challenged and evicted whenever they are encountered by the minister of the gospel.

In this chapter we will talk about how to cast out demons who have invaded the bodies and lives of the people we encounter in gospel ministry. Before we discuss how to cast out demons, however, we will first look into the Bible to discover just who the demons are, and how they afflict and possess their victims.

Chapter 12: How to Cast Out Demons

UNDERSTANDING OUR ENEMIES

Who are the Demons?

The Existence of Demons. Bible scholars sometime disagree concerning the origin of demons. Some say they are the disembodied spirits of some pre-adamic race. Others more convincingly argue that, according to the biblical evidence, demons are angels who sinned and fell with Satan in his rebellion against God (Matt. 25:41; Rev. 12:9). One thing we can be absolutely sure of is their existence; the Bible leaves no doubt about that. We can also be certain of their work, that is, oppose the work of God on every hand. That work, according Wilbur O'Donovan, includes giving "power to sinful human beings (like witches) who seek supernatural power over other people."[1] Jesus often confronted and cast out demons. He then told us that we, His church, would be involved in the same ministry (Mark 16:17; Luke 9:1-2).

Characteristics of Demons. What are demons like? What is their nature and character? The Bible teaches the following things about the nature and character of demons:

- They are actual living beings (Luke 4:33-35; 8:28-31; Acts 16:16-17; James 2:19). They are not some impersonal force, either real or imagined. They are actual beings with individual intellects, wills, and personalities.
- They are spirits (Gen. 3:1; Rev. 16:13). As unembodied spirits they seek to dwell in the bodies of people.
- They are powerful. They have intelligence, strength, and power (Luke 8:29; Acts 16:16-17; 2 Thess. 2:9). They are, however, limited in power. Unlike God, who is uncreated and all powerful, they are created beings with finite power. They are in no way a match for the power of God.
- They are morally perverted and evil (Mark 1:23; Eph. 6:12). They are utterly steeped and confirmed in sin. They are absolutely evil, cruel, and malignant.

---

[1] William O. Donovan, Jr., *Introduction to Biblical Christianity from an African Perspective,* (Ilorin, Nigeria: Nigeria Evangelical Fellowship, 1992), 235.

Chapter 12: How to Cast Out Demons

Demonic Objectives. Just as Christians seek to fulfill the will of their Heavenly Father, demons seek to fulfill the will of their father, the devil. One of Satan's primary objectives is to strike out at God and hurt Him, and the demons share his ambition. Knowing that they cannot stand against God, nor hurt Him directly, Satan and his demons seek to hurt God indirectly by wounding and crippling the ones whom God loves—the human race. Therefore, a key objective of the demons is to strike out against man (and, therefore, against God) by gaining access to man's body, soul, and spirit. They do this in at least three ways:

- By seeking man's worship (1 Cor. 10:19-21). Thus they deny God the worship that He is rightfully due.
- By seeking to hold man in bondage to fear, sickness, and enslaving habits. In this way they deface the image of God in man.
- By blinding men to the truth of the gospel (Acts 10:38; 2 Cor. 4:4; 2Tim. 2:25; Heb. 2:14). They thus keep men from a living relationship with God both in time and in eternity.

O'Donovan identifies several types of activities in which demons engage. I have listed seven of them with comments:

- *Deception.* Through lies, demons promote hatred, false religion, and false teachings in the church (John 8:44; 1 Tim. 4:1; 2 Pet. 2:21).
- *Murder and violence.* If left to carry out their twisted desires, demons bring violence, harm, and sometimes death to their victims (John 8:44).
- *Torture.* Demons torture people by afflicting them with blindness (Matt. 12:22), dumbness (Matt..12:22), deformity (Luke 13:11-17); physical sickness (Job 2:7, Acts 10:38), and mental madness (Luke 8:27-29).
- *Sexual uncleanness.* The Bible often speaks of "unclean spirits" referring to their moral uncleanness and to the uncleanness they kindle in their human hosts (Matt.10:1; Mark 1:23; 3:11).

- *Hindrances to the work of the gospel*. As we have already mentioned above, demons seek to oppose the advance of the gospel at every opportunity (Eph. 6:12; 1 Thess. 2:18).
- *General harassment of the people of God* (Luke 22:31; 2 Cor. 12:7). Demons seek to harass, trouble, disturb, frustrate, and discourage the people of God whenever they can.
- *Promoting idolatry and witchcraft* (Deut. 32:16-17; 1 Sam. 15:23). It is often demons who are in the background controlling and empowering much of the witchcraft, idolatry, and ancestor worship we see in our world today (1 Cor. 10:19-20).[2]

Demonic Possession

Demons seek to afflict and control their victims in a number of ways. The most severe form of demonic affliction is called demon possession in our Bibles. When a demon (or demons) possesses an individual, he enters into that individual and takes control of his or her life. This control can be either partial or entire. It can be either continual or occasional. Demon possession affects its victims in many tragic ways including the following:

- Personality changes, or a clouding of consciousness (Mark 9:26)
- Another personality speaking through the afflicted person (Luke 8:28-30)
- Great physical strength (Luke 8:29)
- Unexplained knowledge or occultic powers (Acts 16:16-17)
- Severe physical disturbances (Mark 1:26), including deaf-mutism and blindness (Matt. 12:22-30; 9:32-34)
- Suicidal and self-destructive tendencies (Mark 9:22, 5:5)
- Reaction to, and fear of Christ or His name (Mark 1:24).

Some teach that a Christian can be possessed by a demon. Others deny this. So, what is the truth? Can a Christian be demon

---

[2]O'Donovan, 231-235.

possessed? No, a Christian cannot be possessed by a demon. Although a Christian can be tempted, deceived, attacked, and even oppressed by demons from the outside, it is impossible for a Christian to be possessed (that is, inhabited by and taken control of at will) by a demon. There are four facts that lend support to this view: First, in the New Testament there is no recorded instance of a born-again believer ever being demon possessed or having a demon cast out of him. Secondly, in Scripture there are ample grounds for believing that deliverance from demons often happened at conversion.[3] Thirdly, in none of the epistles does demon possession appear as a danger to which Christians are exposed, or about which Christians are warned. And finally, we should remember that although a Christian cannot be demon-possessed, possession is possible in the backslider or apostate. Many, in my experience, who claim to have dealt with demon possessed Christians were in fact dealing with backsliders or apostates from the faith.

Satan, A Defeated Foe

In confronting demons it is important that we keep two powerful truths in focus. First, we must never forget that the power of the devil in this age is severely restrained by the presence of the Holy Spirit (2 Thess. 2:7). Through the power of the Spirit we have commanding power over demons. Second, we must not forget that the power of Satan and his demons was broken at Calvary (John 12:31). Paul said, "And having disarmed the powers and authorities, he [Jesus] made a public spectacle of them, triumphing over them by the cross" (Col. 2:15). The powers and authorities spoken of in this verse are demonic and satanic powers. At the cross Jesus broke the back of Satan. Satan and his demons are now defeated enemies because of Christ's mighty work at Calvary!

---

[3]Note especially the biblical account of Philip's revival in Samaria in Acts 8:5-8.

HOW TO CAST OUT DEMONS

Before we discuss how to cast out demons, let's first talk about the deliverance minister himself.

The Deliverance Minister
There are certain essential things anyone wanting to be involved in deliverance ministry must know and do. Listed below are five essential requisites for the deliverance minister:

1. He or she must understand that the casting out of demons is an actual battle with real, malignant foes, and the fight must never be taken lightly.
2. Because the battle will be a spiritual one, it is particularly important that the one ministering deliverance be filled with the Holy Spirit.
3. The deliverance minister must be submitted entirely to the will of God (James 4:7).
4. He or she must have a thorough knowledge of their spiritual armor (Eph. 6:10-18), and they must know how to appropriate and use it in battle.
5. He or she must have a living faith in the victory of Calvary, the blood Christ, and the authority vested in Him.

Ministering Deliverance from Demons
We, as the ministers of Christ, have been commissioned and equipped to minister deliverance to those who are oppressed by demonic forces. Remember, Jesus is our example and guide in such spiritual warfare (Luke 4:18-19; 31-37; Acts 10:38), and He has commissioned us to follow Him into the battle (Mark 16:15-18).

Not only has Jesus commissioned us, He has also equipped us to minister deliverance to the oppressed. Through the infilling and gifts of the Holy Spirit we have been given the means to expose and reveal demons. We have also been given power and authority to use His name to command and expel them (Luke 9:1-2; 10:17-19).

Chapter 12: How to Cast Out Demons

The Process of Deliverance

The expulsion of demons and the breaking of demonic bondages is the work of God through the authority of Jesus' name and the power of the Holy Spirit. It is both a sign of the presence of the kingdom of God and a demonstration of the power and lordship of Christ over His world. As in healing the sick, the following three elements are generally involved in demonic deliverance:

1. Interview (Discovery). If an interview is possible—and this is not always the case—then it is the obvious first step in the deliverance process. It is during this discovery stage that we may, through the gift of discerning of spirits, discover the demonic presence. Also, sometimes demons, when agitated by the presence of God, will expose themselves as they often did in the ministry of Jesus (Mark 1:23; 5:6-7).

Before the actual deliverance begins, it is often good, when possible, to demand a commitment from the one seeking deliverance. Lead him or her in a prayer of repentance and confession of sin, especially those sins that are closely related to his spiritual bondage. Here the candidate must boldly renounce the demonic infestation, and the accompanying works of the flesh in his or her life.

2. Ministry Engagement. At this point, the minster will move into the actual power encounter with the demonic forces. He or she may choose to begin by calling on Jesus and for the Holy Spirit to come. Once he senses the manifest presence of God, he can then proceed to casting out (or in some cases, driving away) the demons. One or more of the following procedures may be used:

- He may bind the demons in the name of Jesus (Matt. 16:17-19; 18:18).
- He may command the demons to come out, be gone, or loose their hold (Luke 4:35).
- He may also command the demons not to reenter (Mark 9:25).

Sometimes there will be struggle or resistance on the part of the demons (Luke 8:29; 11:14). In such cases the deliverance minister should persist in faith until the victory comes. Deliverance

Chapter 12: How to Cast Out Demons

is often accompanied by physical manifestations (Mark 7:30; Luke 4:33-35; 9:42). In such cases the minister should not be intimidated or distracted by such manifestations, but he should continue to move in the power of the Spirit, order the demons to be quiet (Mark 1:25;34), and in the authority he has in Christ, command them to come out and stay out (Mark 9:25).

Don Stamps cites seven elements involved in delivering people from demonic bondage:

- Recognize that we are not in a conflict against flesh and blood but against spiritual forces and powers of evil (Eph. 6:12).
- Live before God, fervently committed to his truth and righteousness (Rom. 12:1-2; Eph. 6:14).
- Have faith that Satan's power can be broken in any specific area of his domain (Acts 26:11; Eph. 6:16; 1 Thess. 5:8), and realize that the believer has powerful spiritual weapons given by God for the destruction of Satan's strongholds (2 Cor. 10:4-5).
- Proclaim the gospel of the kingdom in the fullness of the Holy Spirit (Matt. 4:23; Luke 1:15-17; Acts 1:8, 2:4, 8:12; Rom. 1:16; Eph. 6:15).
- Challenge Satan and his power directly by believing in Jesus' name (Acts 16:16-18), by using God's Word (Eph. 6:17), by praying in the Spirit (Acts 6:4; Eph. 6:18), by fasting ... and by driving out demons (see Matt. 10:1, note; 12:28; 17:17-21; Mark 16:17; Luke.10:17; Acts 5:16; 8:7; 16:18; 19:12).
- Pray especially for the Holy Spirit to convict the lost concerning sin, righteousness and the coming judgment (John 16:7-11).
- Pray for and eagerly desire the manifestation of the Spirit through gifts of healing, tongues, miracles, signs and wonders (Acts 4:29-33; 10:38; 1 Cor. 12:7-11).[4]

---

[4] Don Stamps, "Power Over Satan and Demons" in *The Full Life Study Bible,* KJV (Grand Rapids: Zondervan, 1992), 1486.

Chapter 12: How to Cast Out Demons

3. Post-prayer Guidance. The final step in the deliverance encounter is post-prayer guidance and counsel. When a person has been under the control or strong influence of demons, follow-up counseling and prayer support is vital. The person will need much prayer, counsel, and emotional support. This, then, is not the time to abandon this person; it is the time to show him or her loving concern. It is also essential that we immediately determine his spiritual condition. If he is not born again, he should immediately be lead into the salvation experience. We should also see that the person is immediately led into the experience of the baptism in the Holy Spirit. Jesus sternly warned about neglecting these essential matters:

> When an evil spirit comes out of a man, it goes through arid places seeking rest and does not find it. Then it says "I will return to the house I left." When it arrives, it finds the house unoccupied, swept clean and put in order. Then it goes and takes with it seven other spirits more wicked that itself, and they go in and live there. And the final condition of that man is worse than the first... (Matt. 12:43-45)

Further, it is important that the person's unresolved emotional and spiritual problems be dealt with. The minister and other mature Christians should maintain close contact with the person until he or she is completely free from their bondage.

As ministers of the gospel we have been commissioned to cast out demons. We must do this in the power and anointing of the Spirit, and in a way that shows loving concern for the dignity of the people to whom we are ministering. Our chief concern, however, should not be chasing demons but the proclamation of the life changing gospel of Christ!

FOR REFLECTION AND REVIEW

1. In the gospel of Mark what was Jesus' first recorded miracle? According to Mark's version of Jesus' Great Commission, what is the first sign to follow believers?
2. State two differing views concerning the origin of demons? In your opinion which view is the most biblical?

Chapter 12: How to Cast Out Demons

3. What one thing concerning demons can we be absolutely certain about?
4. List four characteristics of demons.
5. What is Satan's primary objective? How does he seek to carry out this objective?
6. List three ways demons strike out at God and man.
7. List seven types of activities in which demons engage.
8. What is the most severe form of demonization? Describe it.
9. List seven ways in which demonic possession may affect its victims.
10. Can a Christian be demon possessed? Give scriptural reasons to support your answer.
11. State two important truths we should remember when we are called upon to confront demonic powers.
12. List five essential requisites for a deliverance minister.
13. What commission has Jesus given us about dealing with demons? What equipment has He given us that we might defeat them?
14. What are we trying to discover during the interview stage of a demonic deliverance?
15. If possible, what should we lead the seeker of deliverance to do before we begin the ministry engagement?
16. What three scriptural procedures can the deliverance minister use in casting out demons.
17. What do we do if the demons resist our attempts to cast them out?
18. Reread the seven steps for casting out demons mentioned in *The Full Life Study Bible* (later called the *Life in the Spirit Study Bible*). Discuss the ones that seem particularly important to you.
19. Why is post-prayer counsel so important in dealing with the demon possessed?
20. If the person delivered is not saved or baptized in the Holy Spirit, what should the deliverance minister do once the person is delivered? Why?
21. Review this chapter and then list the three steps involved in casting out demons.

– CHAPTER 13 –

How To Pray
with believers to be
Filled
with the Spirit

Being baptized in the Holy Spirit is an essential experience in the life of every believer—especially if he or she desires to be used in power ministry. In Chapter 6 we discussed how a person may personally receive the gift of the Holy Spirit. In this chapter we will take our discussion a step further; we will talk about how to lead others into this vital Christian experience.

We will do this by recommending a practical "how to" model for praying with people to receive the Holy Spirit. The author has used this model of praying for people both in the United States and in Africa and has personally seen hundreds of people filled with the Spirit.

PRELIMINARY CONSIDERATIONS

Anyone desiring to help others be filled with the Spirit must understand three basic truths: First, he must understand who can be filled with the Spirit. Next, he must understand who can pray with others to be filled with the Spirit. Finally, it is useful to know four essential qualities needed for one to receive the Holy Spirit. Let's examine these important matters.

Chapter 13: How to Pray with Believers to Be Filled with the Spirit

Who Can Be Filled with the Spirit?

Anyone who has been truly born again can and should immediately be filled with the Holy Spirit. This vital experience is not just for special Christians who have reached a certain level of holiness or spiritual maturity in their lives. Nor is it only for a certain class of people belonging to a particular church group or denomination. The promise is for all Christians of all ages (Acts 2:17, 18; 38-39).

Who Can Pray with Others to Be Filled with the Spirit?

Anyone who has himself or herself been filled with the Spirit can lead someone else into this marvelous experience. The chief requirement in praying for others to be filled with the Spirit is a sincere desire to see others blessed and used by God.

Elements Involved in Receiving the Holy Spirit

It is helpful for the Christian worker to understand five important spiritual elements involved in a person's being filled with the Holy Spirit: desire, faith, prayer, obedience, and yieldedness to God. Let's look briefly at each of these elements:

1. Desire. The Bible often stresses the importance of desire in seeking after God. God once said to Israel, "You will seek me and find me when you seek me with all your heart" (Jer. 29:13). Jesus said, "Blessed are those who hunger and thirst for righteousness, for they will be filled" (Matt. 5:6; cf. John 7:37). In another place, while teaching on how to receive the Holy Spirit, He said, "Seek [literally, "keep on seeking"] and you will find" (Luke 11:9). Persistent seeking is a fruit of desire. The seeker must know that God will only give His Spirit to those who ardently seek His face.

2. Faith. Faith is the prime ingredient for receiving anything from God, including the Holy Spirit. Paul reminded the Galatian Christians that they had received the Holy Spirit, not by the works of the law, but "by believing what [they] heard" (Gal. 3:2). Jesus said that the Spirit would flow through "whoever believes in me" (John 7:38). One aim of the person leading others into the baptism in the Holy Spirit must therefore be to inspire faith in the heart of the seeker. We will speak more about this later.

3. Prayer. The Holy Spirit is given in answer to believing prayer. Jesus said, "Ask, and it will be given to you…" (Luke

11:9). In another place He taught, "Whatever you ask for in prayer, believe that you have received it, and it will be yours" (Mark 11:24). When Jesus was anointed by the Spirit, He was praying (Luke 3:21-22). Before the disciples received the Spirit at Pentecost, "they all joined together constantly in prayer" (Acts 1:14). Before Paul was filled with the Spirit he spent time in prayer (Acts 9:11). Anyone desiring to be filled with the Spirit must earnestly seek God's face in prayer.

4. *Obedience.* An obedient heart is essential in receiving the Holy Spirit. Peter said that God gives the Holy Spirit "to those who obey him" (Acts 5:32). He was talking specifically about those who will obey God and preach the gospel (vv. 29-32). The primary purpose for receiving the Holy Spirit is to receive power to witness (Acts 1:8). God is ready to empower those who are ready to obey His command to share the gospel with the lost.

5. *Yieldedness to God.* Yieldedness to God is another vital element in receiving the Holy Spirit. Just as one being baptized in water yields himself completely to the pastor, the one bing baptized in the Holy Spirit must yield himself completely to Jesus. He should, therefore, be instructed to yield his entire being to the Lord. This yieldedness should include spirit, mind, and body (Rom. 6:13; 12:1). It is through such yieldedness that the Holy Spirit will fill the person, take control of his being, and begin to speak through him in other tongues.

THE PROCEDURE: HOW TO PRAY WITH BELIEVERS TO BE FILLED WITH THE HOLY SPIRIT

As we did in the chapters on healing the sick and casting out demons, we suggest a three-step model in praying with believers to receive the Holy Spirit, including interview, prayer engagement, and post-prayer guidance.

Step 1: The Interview

In the initial interview process we seek to accomplish four things: First we seek to establish rapport with the candidate. That is, we seek to build an initial warm relationship with him. Next, we seek to affirm and inspire the candidate's faith. Third, We seek to discover the candidate's level of desire for God, as well as his

Chapter 13: How to Pray with Believers to Be Filled with the Spirit

spiritual condition. Finally, we seek to instruct the seeker as to what he must do to be filled with the Spirit.

1. Establishing Rapport. The first goal in the interview process is to establish rapport[5] with the candidate. If you already know the person, this is, of course, unnecessary. However, if you are not acquainted with the candidate, begin by introducing yourself. Say, "Hello, my name is _____. What is your name?" Listen closely to what the candidate has to say. Repeat his name back to him, and then use his name during your time of ministry.

2. Affirmation and Inspiration. Next, seek to the affirm[6] the candidate and to inspire his faith. You might say, "I am so glad you came to receive the Spirit; you did the right thing." You could also say, "This could be one of the greatest days of your life. God has a very special gift for you." Remember, the candidate is probably nervous at this point. These words will help set him at ease and prepare his heart to receive the Holy Spirit.

3. Discovery. One goal at this point is to find out why the seeker has come forward, and to discover precisely where he is in his spiritual experience. You might ask such questions as follows:

- "What do you want God to do for you today?" or "Did you come to be filled with the Spirit?" Don't assume he has come to be filled with the Spirit; he may have come for another reason. If he has come to be filled, it is good for him to say so. Doing this will strengthen his resolve to be filled.
- "Have you ever been filled before?" If the candidate has been filled before, he may need little more than brief encouragement to be refilled. If he has never been filled, he needs more instruction.

---

[5]To establish rapport (pronounced ra-poor) with a person means to begin a relationship with him. It means that we begin to be comfortable in one another's presence.

[6]To affirm someone is to say things to him that will make him feel good about himself and what he has done.

Chapter 13: How to Pray with Believers to Be Filled with the Spirit

- "Have you ever seen anyone filled with the Spirit?" If he has seen others filled with the Spirit, he may have a good idea of what will happen to him. If not, he will need a more detailed explanation.

Once you have asked these questions, listen very closely to his response. These discoveries will help you to know how to proceed to the next step.

4. Instruction. At this point in the interview process we have two primary goals: (1) to stir up expectant faith in the heart of the candidate; and (2) to bring to an accurate understanding of what he must do to be filled and what they can expect to happen.[7]

One way to encourage faith is to remind the seeker of God's promises concerning the Holy Spirit. Assure him that, if he is truly born again, God is ready now to fill him with the Holy Spirit. Remind him of the promise of Jesus: "Ask and it will be given you ... everyone who asks receives" (Luke 11:9-10). The seeker must believe that God will, the moment he asks, fill him with His Spirit. This is what we call "expectant faith." The seeker should, therefore, expect to be filled with the Spirit, and expect to speak with other tongues as the Spirit gives him utterance. Further, he should be prepared to act on that expectation. In addition, he should be made aware of the fact that, once he is filled with the Spirit, he will be given power and boldness to be Christ's witness (Acts 1:8; 4:31).

Next, you will seek to bring the candidate to an accurate understanding about what he must do to be filled, and what he can expect to happen as he is being filled. He needs to know that being filled with the Holy Spirit is not a difficult nor extraordinary thing for a believer. It is, in fact, the normal thing for a Christian to do. He should know that he will not be filled with "another Holy Spirit" but the same Holy Spirit who already indwells him since his new birth.

You can tell the seeker, "Receiving the Holy Spirit is easy! It is the natural thing to do. In fact, for the born again Christian, it is

---

[7] Many of these instructions could, of course, be given in a sermon preceding this time of ministry.

Chapter 13: How to Pray with Believers to Be Filled with the Spirit

as easy as breathing." And it's true! Remember what Jesus did with His disciples: "He breathed on [or into] them and said, 'Receive the Holy Spirit'" (John 20:22). Receiving the Holy Spirit is much like breathing. Just as breathing is the natural thing for a person to do, receiving the Holy Spirit is the natural thing for the child of God to do.

Next, let the candidate know exactly what you plan to do and what will happen to him. You could say something like this:

> First, we will pray together. Then, I will lead you in a prayer in which we will ask the Lord to come and baptize us in the Holy Spirit. The Lord will hear and answer our prayer. I know He will because we will be praying according to His will (1 John 5:14). At this point you should be very sensitive to the Spirit. You will sense His coming upon you.
>
> After this, I will ask you to take a step of faith and receive the Holy Spirit. I will lead you in another short prayer. It will go something like this, "Right now, in the name of Jesus, I receive the Holy Spirit." Then, by faith, you will "believe that you have received" (Mark 11:24). The instant you believe, the Holy Spirit will fill you. You will sense His Presence deep within—in your innermost being.
>
> You will then begin to speak, not from your mind, but from your spirit, where you sense the Presence of God inside. As you speak, you will begin to say words you don't understand. When this happens, don't be afraid, just continue to speak. God is filling you with His Spirit!

Then ask, "Do you have any question? Are you ready to be filled with the Spirit?" If the seeker has questions, answer them. If he has no questions proceed to the prayer engagement.

Prayer Engagement

In the prayer engagement we do two things: (1) We lead the candidate in a prayer asking for the Holy Spirit, and (2) we lead the candidate in his step of faith in receiving the Holy Spirit.

1. Lead the Seeker in Prayer. Much as you would lead a sinner in the sinner's prayer, you now lead the new believer in a prayer asking to be filled with the Spirit. The prayer may proceed as follows, with the candidate repeating each line:

Chapter 13: How to Pray with Believers to Be Filled with the Spirit

> Lord I come now to be filled with the Holy Spirit ... You promised that I would receive power when I received the Spirit ... I need that power to be your witness ... Right now, there is nothing in my life I want more ... You have promised that everyone who asks, receives ... I am asking; therefore, I expect to receive ... When I begin to speak, I will release my faith ... I will not be afraid ... I will begin to pray in tongues as Your Spirit gives me utterance.

After you have prayed, assure the candidate that God has heard his prayer, and that He is ready now to fill him with the Spirit. Encourage the candidate to be spiritually sensitive to the presence of the Spirit who will come upon Him. You may want to take a few moments to quietly worship the Lord together, responding to His presence.

2. Lead the Seeker in His Step of Faith. You may now ask the seeker to lift his hands toward heaven and pray this simple prayer of faith with you, "Lord, right now, in Jesus Name, I receive the Holy Spirit." This prayer provides a definite point where the seeker can focus his faith to receive the Holy Spirit. He should, at that moment, "truly believe that he has received." The moment he believes, the Spirit will come and fill him. Encourage him to be aware the Spirit's coming into his spirit. He will sense Spirit's presence deep inside.

He should now act in bold faith and begin to speak, not from his mind, but from deep within, from where he senses God's Spirit inside. As he yields to the Spirit flowing into and through his being, he will begin to speak words he does not understand. This speaking will not be a forced effort, but a natural flow of supernatural words. Encourage him not to be fearful but to cooperate fully with the Spirit by boldly speaking out in faith.

If the candidate does not soon begin to speak in tongues, encourage him to continue yielding his being to the Lord. You may want to worship with him, allowing the Lord to refill you with the Holy Spirit. This will often provide encouragement to the candidate to keep seeking until he too is filled.

If the seeker seems to have difficulty responding to the Lord, it is sometimes helpful to repeat the above procedure. As you do,

Chapter 13: How to Pray with Believers to Be Filled with the Spirit

point out how the seeker may more perfectly respond to the Spirit. Once the he begins to speak in tongues, encourage him to continue on. Remain with him as long as he continues to pray in the Spirit.

Post-prayer Guidance

As with prayer for the sick and deliverance from demons, it is important that post-prayer counseling be given to the candidate. If he is filled with the Spirit you will give one kind of counsel; if he is not, you will give another kind.

If the Candidate is Filled With the Spirit. If the candidate is filled with the Spirit and speaks in tongues, the following advice is appropriate: Tell him that receiving the Spirit is not an end in itself; it is a means to an end. The purpose for receiving the Spirit is that we may receive power for life and service. You may want to say, "This is not the end; it's just the beginning. God will now begin to use you in a new and powerful way. Expect to have new power in your life. Go out right now and tell someone about Jesus." You will want to add, "You should also spend time each day praying in the Spirit (that is, in tongues). This will give you strength and will remind you of the Spirit's presence in your life."

If the Candidate is Not Filled With the Spirit. If he is not filled with the Spirit, you will want to give the following advice and encouragement: Tell him to not be discouraged because he did not receive the Holy Spirit at this time. Assure him that the promise of Jesus is still true: "Everyone who asks receives" (Luke 11:10). Tell him that he should keep asking and he will receive, keep seeking and he will find, and to keep knocking and the door will be opened unto him (literal translation of Luke 11:9). You may want to ask him if he would like to pray again. If he does, repeat the above procedure, encouraging him to act in bold faith.

OTHER IMPORTANT CONSIDERATIONS

As we conclude this chapter we will mention three other things worthy of consideration when leading others into the baptism in the Holy Spirit:

Chapter 13: How to Pray with Believers to Be Filled with the Spirit

Know What the Bible Says on the Subject

First, if one is going to help others be filled with the Spirit, it stands to reason that he should seek to know all he can on the subject. Most importantly, he should study the Word of God, especially the book of Acts, to see what it says on the subject. Also, he could read and study good books on the subject. The more one knows about the Holy Spirit and His work in the lives of people, the better able he will be to help others experience His power.

Don't Let Spiritual Laziness Disqualify You

Next, if you would help people receive the Spirit of God, then don't let spiritual laziness disqualify you. Because it is often hard work to pray with people to be filled with the Spirit, some shy away from preaching on the subject and seeking to lead others into the experience. If that is the case with you, repent of your spiritual laziness, and give yourself wholeheartedly to this vital ministry.

Watch Your Intensity Level

Finally, when praying with others to be filled with the Spirit, it is important that you watch your intensity level. By this I mean you should be upbeat and positive when praying with them. Let your enthusiasm show! At the same time you should beware of being too pushy. Wisdom will show you the right balance between intensity and reserve in encouraging people to be filled with the Spirit.

In this lesson we have talked about how you can be effective in leading people into the baptism in the Holy Spirit. We hope that you will now dedicate yourself to the task. There is nothing more satisfying than helping others personally experience the Spirit's power and presence.

FOR REFLECTION AND REVIEW

1. Who can be filled with the Spirit?
2. Who can pray with others to be filled with the Spirit?

Chapter 13: How to Pray with Believers to Be Filled with the Spirit

3. Why do we say that desire is an important element in one's receiving the Holy Spirit?
4. What should be a primary aim of the one seeking to lead others into Spirit baptism?
5. What do we mean when we say that the one seeking to be filled with the Spirit must yield himself or herself to God?
6. List five elements involved in a person's being filled with the Holy Spirit.
7. What four things does the minister seek to accomplish during the interview stage?
8. What can the one ministering do to help establish rapport with the one who has come to be filled with the Spirit?
9. What can the minister do to affirm the person seeking to be filled with the Spirit?
10. What two things should one discover about the candidate as he proceeds in ministry to that person?
11. What three questions may the minister ask the candidate to discover his or her previous experience in relation to being filled with the Spirit?
12. What are the two primary goals in instructing the candidate at this point?
13. What ways may we use to inspire the faith of the seeker?
14. What things could the minister tell the seeker in order to increase his or her understanding about receiving the Spirit?
15. What two things will the minister seek to do during the prayer engagement time?
16. What points should be covered in leading seekers in his or her prayer asking God to fill them with the Holy Spirit?
17. What actions does the minister take in leading the candidate to take his or her step of faith to receive the Spirit?
18. What should the minister do if the seeker is immediately filled with the Holy Spirit?
19. What should the minister do if the seeker is not immediately filled?
20. What post-prayer guidance should the candidate be given once he has been filled with the Spirit?
21. What post-prayer guidance should the candidate be given if he or she is not filled with the Spirit at this time?
22. How can one come to know more about the subject of the Holy Spirit?

Chapter 13: How to Pray with Believers to Be Filled with the Spirit

23. How can a laziness disqualify someone from praying with others to be filled with the Holy Spirit?
24. What do we mean when we say the minister should watch his or her intensity level when praying with people to be filled with the Holy Spirit? Why is this important?

Chapter 13: How to Pray with Believers to Be Filled with the Spirit

– CHAPTER 14 –

POWER ENCOUNTER IN CAMPAIGN EVANGELISM

In the last three chapters we talked about how to do power ministry from a pastoral point of view. Now we will discuss power ministry from the point of view of a campaign evangelist. The pastor often prays for people one person at a time. The campaign evangelist, however, often prays for people *en masse,* that is, he or she will often pray for many people at one time.

Nevertheless, the things we said about the pastor in Chapter 11 are also true about the campaign evangelist. He should never try to manipulate the results of his prayer time with the people. Like the pastor, he wants the people to feel the love of God as he ministers to them. Therefore, he will never threaten the people. And he will never embarrass them by accusing them of not having enough faith.

He will also be deeply concerned about the spiritual condition of his hearers. After all, that is why he is holding the campaign—he wants to lead people to know Christ as Savior and Lord. He will not become so concerned about showing power that he forgets why he is there.

Most of the methods discussed in the previous three chapters can adapted for use by the campaign evangelist. There are, however, some issues about power ministry that relate specifically to campaign evangelism. In this chapter we will address these issues, including (1) the need for signs and wonders in campaign evangelism, (2) how to minister in power during an evangelistic campaign and (3), leading new believers into the baptism in the Holy Spirit.

THE NEED FOR SIGNS AND WONDERS IN CAMPAIGN EVANGELISM

The New Testament Pattern

The ministries of Jesus and the apostles should serve as a pattern for our ministries today. Jesus said to his disciples: "Come follow me ... and I will make you fishers of men" (Matt. 4:19). Jesus was promising to train them for ministry. He would be their example and they would learn to minister by imitating Him. Jesus also promised them power for ministry (Acts 1:8). Their ministries would be evidenced by the same works that accompanied His ministry. He once told them, "I tell you the truth, anyone who has faith in me will do what I have been doing. He will do even greater things than these, because I am going to the Father" (John 14:12).

A close examination of the ministries of the apostles in the book of Acts proves this fact. They ministered in the same way Jesus did, and their ministries were accompanied by the same miraculous results. We too have been promised that same power that Jesus and those early ministers of the gospel had (Acts 2:38-39). Therefore, we can take their ministries as patterns for our ministries today.

If we are to pattern our ministries after the ministries of Jesus and the apostles, we must answer two important questions: First, "Did Jesus and the apostles do mass evangelism?" And second, "Were signs and wonders present?" The answer to both questions is "Yes." Note three things about the ministries of Jesus and the apostles:

1. Jesus and the apostles often ministered to large gatherings of people. The word "multitude" or "multitudes" appears 83 times in the gospels and 21 times in Acts (KJV). Also, the phrase "much people" appears 14 times in the gospels and Acts. Most of these references speak of the crowds who were attending the ministry of Jesus and the apostles.

Chapter 14: Power Encounter in Campaign Evangelism

2. *Jesus and the apostles performed miracles in the presence these crowds.* Jesus performed His signs publicly. The apostles also preached and performed miraculous signs in public settings. Paul reminded king Agrippa that their ministries were not "done in a corner" (Acts 26:26). They were done publicly and before many people. The term often used for these public miracles is "signs and wonders" (Matt.15:29; Luke 9:37-43; 11:14; John 20:30; Acts 2:22; 2:43; 3:10; 4:30; 5:12; 6:8; 7:36; 8:6, 13; 14:3; Rom. 15:12,19; 2 Cor. 12:12; Heb. 2:3-4).

3. *Jesus and the apostles always preached the gospel.* Jesus and the apostles did not perform miracles simply for show. The miracles were done to point to the truth of the gospel. They always preached the gospel. Along with the miracles they performed, they called the people to repentance and faith.

How Signs and Wonders Benefit Campaign Evangelism

Signs and wonders can benefit campaign evangelism in four important ways:

1. They attract people. A miracle attracts attention to the campaign and to the gospel that is being preached there. This happened when the crippled man was healed at the Gate Beautiful: "All the people were astonished and came running to them..." (Acts 3:11). Peter used this miracle as an opportunity to preach the gospel (3:12–26). As a result, many were saved (4:4). The same things occurred in Philip' ministry in Samaria (8:6).

2. They illustrate God's character and compassion. When people see a sick person healed or a demoniac delivered, they are made to know the compassion of God. They see how God cares about their own hurts and pains. This makes them want to follow a God who will help them in their times of need.

3. They display Christ's power over false gods. When people see a person delivered from a demon or a curse, they are made to realize that God is stronger than the devil, their gods, or ancestral spirits. They see that Christianity is more powerful than their own false religion.

4. Prepare listeners to believe. When people see God perform a miracle in a campaign, it makes them ready to believe the gospel. A "faith shift" takes place in their hearts, as discussed in Chapter

4. They are ready to respond when the invitation is given to receive Christ.

Sometimes, a miracle performed in a private setting can have great impact on a public meeting. Peter healed Aeneas and raised Dorcas a private settings; however, both miracles resulted in a widespread response to the gospel (Acts 9:32-43). At times, an evangelist will be invited to a home to pray for someone there. Whenever possible, the evangelist should go. A miracle in a home could be the key to a great harvest of souls.

An Important Reemphasis

An important truth must be reemphasized here. The campaign evangelist must never forget that his primary task in the campaign is preaching the gospel. Christ must be clearly and powerfully proclaimed. While miracles can point to Christ, only a clear presentation of the gospel can tell people how to be saved. Truth encounter must always accompany power encounter (see Chapters 1 and 4). In fact, the preaching itself can also be a demonstration of the presence and power of God. When the preacher is anointed by the Holy Spirit, the people can encounter the power of God in his or her very words.

HOW TO MINISTER IN POWER DURING AN EVANGELISTIC CAMPAIGN

Preparing for the Evangelistic Campaign

A number of things must be done before a campaign begins. Three of these are as follows:

1. Spiritual preparation. If the evangelist hopes to see a demonstration of God's power in the campaign meetings, he must concern himself with spiritual preparation. He should spend time alone in prayer and fasting. He should also pray and fast with the campaign team. For everyone involved in the campaign, this should be a time of personal submission and commitment to the will of the Lord.

2. Strategic prayer warfare. The campaign team should also spend time together in "strategic prayer warfare." Specifically, they should pray for an outpouring of the Holy Spirit upon the campaign. The team could also come against controlling demons

Chapter 14: Power Encounter in Campaign Evangelism

who may be opposing the spread of the gospel in the campaign area (2 Cor. 4:4). If possible, the team should travel to the place where the campaign will be held. There, they can pray with believers in their homes. Team members can also take prayer walks through the area, praying for a move of the Spirit. Prayer walks also offer opportunities for personal evangelism prior to the start of the campaign.

3. Training altar workers. Training altar workers should be done before the start of a campaign. These are the people who will pray with those who come forward during the campaign. They should be trained to lead people to Christ and to do follow-up. Altar workers should also be trained for power ministry. This book could serve as a training manual for them.

Conducting the Evangelistic Campaign

The evangelist will want the power of God to be present in his campaign. Therefore, in conducting the campaign, he must address three critical issues:

1. The spiritual atmosphere. As discussed in Chapter 11, the spiritual atmosphere during the campaign should be characterized by expectant faith and the manifest presence of God. This atmosphere can be aided by prayer and worship. The faith-filled words spoken by those participating in the service can also help to create an atmosphere of expectant faith.

2. Anointing of the Holy Spirit. Those attending the campaign should sense the anointing of the Spirit upon the ministry team. Holiness, prayer, and yieldedness to the Spirit are key spiritual elements in maintaining the anointing upon one's life and ministry.

3. Time for power ministry. In every campaign service time should be given for power ministry to occur. This includes the release of spiritual gifts, prayer for the sick, and the casting out of demons, when necessary. The evangelist should also allow the Holy Spirit to demonstrate His power at any time during the service.

Biblical Methods of Power Ministry

As previously mentioned, Jesus and the apostles are models for our ministries today. We are to use the same methods they used. As we are anointed by the Spirit, we, too, can be used to heal the sick.

Chapter 14: Power Encounter in Campaign Evangelism

Like Jesus, we can do this by speaking a word, giving a command of faith, laying on of hands, releasing spiritual power, or by using any other method found in the New Testament.

It is therefore very important that the evangelist be totally yielded to the Holy Spirit at all times. He or she must listen for the Spirit's voice speaking to their spirits. The Spirit will direct the evangelist on how to minister in any given situation. The campaign evangelist has available all the spiritual weapons discussed in Chapter 10. He should not fail to use these powerful weapons.

Applying the Three-Step Method to Campaign Evangelism

In the preceding three chapters we discussed a three-step method of power ministry. With some slight adjustments, this method can also be used in campaign evangelism.

1. Interview (Discovery). Since time is often limited during a campaign, the evangelist will seldom be able to interview everyone who comes forward for ministry. Even so, he should not neglect the discovery stage of the ministry encounter. To minister effectively to the people, the evangelist must, like Jesus, know what the Father is doing (John 5:19). He or she should, therefore, remain open to the promptings of the Holy Spirit at all times. Sometimes, discovery can be made through revelation gifts (discussed in Chapter 7). The Holy Spirit may reveal to the evangelist special needs in the lives of certain individuals. The Spirit will lead the evangelist as he or she ministers to people.

Also, the evangelist should give instructions before praying for sick people. They should be told what they must do to receive salvation, or deliverance, or healing. The sick should be encouraged to respond in faith to what God is doing. They can also be told what to expect when they are prayed for.

2. Prayer engagement. The evangelist should continue to allow the Holy Spirit to direct him or her during the prayer engagement. Sometimes, he will be directed to pray for people in groups. Occasionally, he might feel led to use a prayer line. At other times, the Holy Spirit may give him a word of knowledge about an individual's need.

The evangelist must be sensitive to the Holy Spirit concerning which healing method to use. The Spirit may direct him to give a

Chapter 14: Power Encounter in Campaign Evangelism

command of faith or to lay hands on the sick. Miraculous results will follow as the evangelist obeys the leading of the Holy Spirit.

The campaign evangelist may also use trained altar workers during the prayer time. These trained workers can effectively pray for those who need healing or deliverance. More personal attention can be given to individuals when this method is used.

3. Post prayer counseling. After the prayer time, the evangelist should instruct those who have responded for prayer. He should encourage them to continue in faith and to immediately testify to others about what God has done for them. The evangelist should also lead to salvation those who have not yet been saved. Some people with acute spiritual needs may need individual counseling and prayer.

LEADING NEW BELIEVERS INTO THE BAPTISM IN THE HOLY SPIRIT

An effective campaign will normally produce a number of new converts. If the work is to be maintained and progress, the evangelist should lead these new believers into the baptism in the Holy Spirit. This is the biblical pattern. In the New Testament Church, new believers were baptized in the Holy Spirit immediately after being saved (Acts 2:38–39; 8:14–17; 9:1-19; 10:44–46; 19:1–6). By being filled with the Spirit, new believers are strengthened in their Christian walk, they are empowered to witness to their family and friends, and they receive power to overcome temptation and stay true to Christ.

Three Methods for Emphasizing the Baptism in the Holy Spirit

How can the campaign evangelist ensure that new converts are baptized in the Holy Spirit? He could use one or all of the following methods:

1. Special prayer times each night. After the campaign has continued for a short time, a number of people will have been saved. The evangelist may plan a special prayer time each night thereafter. New believers would then be invited to pray to receive the Spirit.

2. Holy Spirit-receiving rally. The evangelist may plan a Holy Spirit-receiving rally on one or more evenings during the campaign. He should announce this service early in the campaign, and should encourage new believers to begin preparing their hearts to receive the Holy Spirit. On the night of the rally, the evangelist should preach a sermon on the baptism in the Holy Spirit. He should then pray with believers to be filled with the Spirit at the end of his message.

3. New believers classes. The evangelist may schedule classes for new believers. These classes may be held during the mornings, during the afternoons, or just prior to his evangelistic services each evening. These classes should include clear teaching on the baptism in the Holy Spirit. Prayer for new believers to receive the Holy Spirit should also take place during these sessions.

Nothing is more important for new Christians than being filled with the Holy Spirit. This experience is a key to their continued growth in Christ. It is also the believer's source of power for Christian witness. This experience should not be delayed until a later time; it is too important to ignore. The wise evangelist will not neglect this important spiritual experience.

The Three-Step Method

In Chapter 13, we discussed how to lead one person into the baptism in the Holy Spirit. In a campaign setting, however, the evangelist will often pray with large groups of people to be filled. How can he do this? The evangelist can still use the three-step method. Almost all of the points previously discussed apply. However, the method must be adapted to the campaign situation, as discussed below.

1. The interview. Often, a large group of people will come forward to be filled with the Holy Spirit. In such a case, it is not practical to individually counsel with each person. The wise evangelist can, however, counsel the entire group on how to receive the Holy Spirit. His counsel should include affirming the seekers for coming forward to be filled, teaching them what they must do to be filled, and letting them know what they can expect to happen when they are being filled. He should also seek to inspire their faith to receive the promised gift.

2. Prayer time. During the prayer time, the evangelist should lead the entire group in prayer. This prayer will be very similar to the one discussed in Chapter 13. He should then lead everyone in

Chapter 14: Power Encounter in Campaign Evangelism

their step of faith. The evangelist should not rush the prayer time. He should allow plenty of time for people to seek the Lord and be filled with the Spirit.

3. Post-prayer guidance. When the seekers finish praying, the evangelist should counsel those who have been filled with the Spirit, encouraging them to witness and to walk in the Spirit. He should also encourage those who were not filled with the Spirit. He could tell them to return the next night to seek again for the Holy Spirit. They could also attend classes on the Holy Spirit if they are being offered during the day.

Power ministry is an important part of campaign evangelism. It often opens people's hearts to respond to the gospel and be saved. Those who feel called to campaign evangelism should make it their goal to know how to minister in the power and anointing of the Holy Spirit.

FOR REFLECTION AND REVIEW

1. A campaign evangelist must often pray for people en masse. What does this term mean?
2. What should be the greatest motivation of an evangelist?
3. How can our ministries follow the New Testament ministry pattern?
4. How did Jesus and the apostles use mass evangelism?
5. Where did Jesus and the apostles perform many of their miracles?
6. Why did Jesus and the apostles perform miracles?
7. What is an evangelist's primary responsibility during a campaign?
8. How can preaching demonstrate the presence and power of God?
9. List four ways in which signs and wonders can benefit an evangelistic campaign.
10. Why should a campaign evangelist welcome opportunities to pray for sick people in their homes?
11. In what ways do signs and wonders illustrate the character of God?
12. What can an evangelist do to prepare himself and his team for a coming campaign?

Chapter 14: Power Encounter in Campaign Evangelism

13. What two kinds of "strategic prayer warfare" can be used when preparing for a campaign?
14. How can trained altar workers assist during a campaign meeting?
15. What three things can be done to prepare for an evangelistic campaign?
16. What three important factors should be present in every campaign meeting?
17. When ministering to the sick and demon possessed, what two things should the evangelist do during the "discovery" time.
18. Name at least three methods the campaign evangelist can use to minister to the sick?
19. What counsel should the evangelist give to people after they have received prayer?
20. State at least three reasons the evangelist should lead new converts into the baptism in the Holy Spirit?
21. List three methods an evangelist can use to lead new believers to receive the Spirit.

– APPENDIX 1 –
PART 1
THE HEALING MINISTRY OF JESUS
(THE SYNOPTIC GOSPELS)

Healing Event	Matt.	Mark	Luke	Method Used
1. Man with an evil spirit		1:23	4:33	Exorcism, word
2. Peter's mother-in-law	8:14	1:30	4:38	Touch, word
3. Multitudes	8:16	1:32	4:40	Touch, word, faith
4. Many demons driven out		1:39		Preaching, exorcism
5. A leper	8:2	1:40	5:12	Touch, word, leper's faith, compassion
6. Multitudes			5:15	Response to need
7. A paralytic	9:2	2:3	5:17	Word, friends' faith
8. Man with a shrivelled hand	12:9	3:1	6:6	Word, faith, obedience
9. Multitudes	12:5	3:10		Touch, faith, exorcisms
10. Gadarene demoniac	8:28	5:1	8:26	Word, exorcism
11. Jairus' daughter raised from the dead	9:18	5:22	8:41	Word, touch, father's faith
12. Woman with an issue of blood	9:20	5:25	8:43	touch, power release
13. A few sick people	13:58	6:5		Touch, (Hindered by unbelief).

Appendix 1: The Healing Ministry of Jesus

Healing Event	Matt.	Mark	Luke	Method Used
14. Multitudes	14:34	6:55		Touch, power release
15. Syrophoenician woman's daughter	15:22	7:24		Acknowledgment of faith
16. Deaf and mute man		7:37		Touch, word
17. Blind man		8:22		Touch, gradual healing
18. Boy with an evil spirit	17:14	9:14	9:38	Word, touch, father's faith
19. Blind Bartemaeus	20:30	10:46	18:35	Work, touch, compassion, faith
20. Centurion's servant	8:5		7:2	Response to faith
21. Two blind men	9:27			Word, touch
22. Blind and mute demoniac	12:22		11:14	Exorcism
23. Mute demoniac	9:23			Exorcism
24. Multitudes (Every sickness and disease)	4:23		6:17	Teaching, preaching, healing
25. Multitudes (Every sickness and disease)	9:35			Teaching, preaching, healing
26. Multitudes	11:4		7:21	Not stated
27. Multitudes	14:14		9:11	Compassion
28 Great multitudes (lame, crippled, mute)	15:30			Faith of friends
29. Great multitudes	19:2			Not stated
30. Blind and lame in the Temple	21:14			Response to human need
31. Widow of Nain's son			7:11	Word, touch, compassion
32. Mary Magdalene and others			8:2	Exorcism

Appendix 1: The Healing Ministry of Jesus

Healing Event	Matt.	Mark	Luke	Method Used
33. Woman bound by a demon			13:10	Word, touch
34. Man with dropsy			14:1	Touch
35. Ten lepers			17:11	Command
36. Malcus' ear			22:49	Touch

– APPENDIX 1 –
PART 2
THE HEALING MINISTRY OF JESUS
(THE GOSPEL OF JOHN)

Healing Event	Text	Method Used
37. Nobleman's son	John 4:46	Word, father's faith
38. Impotent man	John 5:2	Word, man's faith
39. Great multitudes	John 6:2	Compassion.
40. Man born blind	John 9:1	Word, touch
41. Lazarus raised from the dead	John 11:1	Command

Note: This chart has been adapted from a chart developed by Jim B. Miller.

Appendix 1: The Healing Ministry of Jesus

– APPENDIX 2 –
THE HEALING METHODS OF CHRIST

You will find in the chart below a list of the various healing methods of Jesus, along with the first-verse location of various examples of Jesus utilizing that particular method. Christ's healing ministry was meant as a model for us to follow (John 20:21; 1 Pet. 2:21; 1 Cor. 11:1).

SPEAKING A WORD: The method Jesus used most often for healing the sick was speaking a word. Sometimes this spoken word was a command to the sick person to do something. Sometimes it was a command to demons to leave. On occasions, Jesus spoke directly to the illness. At other times His word was a simple acknowledgment of the faith of the recipient, or a statement of the fact that the healing had taken place. As you read over the following accounts you will see Jesus speaking a word and healing the sick:

(Mark 1:23; Luke 4:33); (Matt. 8:14, Mark 1:30, Luke 4:38); (Matt. 8:16; Mark 1 32, Luke 4:40); (Matt. 8:2, Mark 1:40, Luke 5:12); (Matt. 9:2, Mark 2:3, Luke 5:17); (Matt. 12:9, Mark 3:1, Luke 6:6); (Matt. 8:28, Mark 5:1, Luke 8:26); (Matt. 9:18, Mark 5:22; Luke 8:41); (Mark 7:32); (Mark 8:22); (Matt. 17:14, Mark 9:14; Luke.9:38); (Matt..20:30, Mark 10:46, Luke 18:35); (Matt..9:27); (Luke 7:11); (Luke 13:10); (Luke 17:11); (John 4:46); (John 5:2); (John 9:1); (John 11:1).

COMMAND OF FAITH: One method Jesus often used to heal the sick was a command of faith. He would command illness to be healed, demons to leave, and the sick to respond with a action of faith. Here are some examples for you to study:

(Matt. 8:14, Mark 1:30, Luke 4:38); (Matt. 9:2, Mark 2:3, Luke 5:17); (Matt. 12:9, Matt. 3:1, Luke 6:6); (Matt. 9:18, Mark 5:22, Luke 8:41); (Mark 7:32); (Matt. 20:30, Mark 10:46, Luke 18:35); (Matt. 9:27); (Luke 7:11): (Luke 13:10); (Luke 7:11); (John 4:46); (John 5:2); (John 9:1); (John 11:1).

Appendix 2: The Healing Methods of Christ

TOUCHING: Jesus often touched people as he healed them. This touching included simply taking the sick person's hand, touching the afflicted where he needed to receive healing, and other forms of touching. Read the following passages to see how Jesus used touching to heal the sick:

(Matt. 8:14, Mark 1:30, Luke 4:38); (Matt. 8:16, Mark 1:32, Luke 4:40); (Matt. 8:2, Mark 1:40; Luke 5:12); (Matt. 9:18; Mark 5:22, Luke 8:41); (Matt. 13:58, Mark 6:5); (Mark 7:32); (Mark 8:22); (Matt. 17:14), (Mark 9:14, Luke 9:38); (Matt. 20:30; Mark 10:46, Luke 18:35); (Matt. 9:27); Luke 13:10); (Luke 14:1); (Luke 22:49); (John 9:1).

THE FAITH OF THE RECIPIENT: Jesus sometimes healed when saw the faith of the person needing healing. Here are some examples:

(Matt. 8:2, Mark 1:40, Luke 5:12); (Matt. 12:15, Mark 3:10); (Matt. 9:20, Mark 5:25, Luke 8:43); (Matt. 20:30, Mark 10:46, Luke 18:35); (Matt. 9:27); (John 5:2).

THE FAITH OF OTHERS: Sometimes Jesus healed when he saw the faith of friends or family members of the ones needing healing:

(Matt. 8:14, Mark 1:30, Luke 4:38); (Matt. 8:16, Mark 1:32, Luke 4:40); (Matt. 9:2, Mark 2:3, Luke 5:17); (Matt. 9:18, Mark 5:22; Luke 8:41); (Matt. 14:34, Mark 6:55); (Matt. 15:22, Mark 7:24); (Mark 7:32); (Mark 8:22); (Matt. 17:14, Mark 9:14, Luke 9:38); (Matt. 8:5, Luke 7:2); (John 4:46).

THE EXPULSION OF DEMONS: Often Jesus would heal the sick by casting out of them the demons that were causing the sickness.

(Mark 1:23, Luke 4:33); (Matt. 12:15, Mark 3:10); (Matt. 8:28, Mark 5:1, Luke 8:26); (Matt. 9:32); (Matt. 12:22, Luke 11:14); (Luke 8:2); (Luke 13:32).

COMPASSION: Compassion for the sick and suffering was an ingredient often found in the healing ministry of Jesus. His compassion caused Him to reach out to them to heal them as follows:

(Matt. 8:2, Mark 1:40, Luke 5:12); (Matt. 20:30, Mark 10:46, Luke 18:35); (Matt. 14:14, Luke 9:11, John 6:2); (Luke 7:11).

Appendix 2: The Healing Methods of Christ

CONFIRMATION OF PREACHING OR TEACHING: Healing was often performed to confirm the message that he taught or preached, as the following passages confirm:

(Mark 1:39); (Matt. 4:25, Luke 6:17); (Matt. 9:35); (Matt. 11:4, Luke 7:21).

EXTRAORDINARY ACTS: Sometimes Jesus healed by using extra-ordinary acts as follows:

(Matt. 9:20, Mark 5:25, Luke 8:43); (Matt. 14:34, Mark 6:55); (Mark 8:22); (John 9:1).

Note: This chart has been adapted from a chart developed by Jim B. Miller

Appendix 2: The Healing Methods of Christ

– BIBLIOGRAPHY –

Bennett, Dennis and Rita. *The Holy Spirit and You.* Plainfield, NJ: Logos International, 1971.

Bonnke, Reinhard. *Mighty Manifestations.* Eastbourne: Kingsway Publications, 1994.

Bosworth, F. F. *Christ the Healer.* Fleming H. Revell Co., 1973.

Burgess, Stanley M. and McGee, Gary B., ed. *Dictionary of Pentecostal and Charismatic Movements.* Grand Rapids, MI: Regency Reference Library, 1988.

Carter, Howard. *Spiritual Gifts and Their Operation.* Springfield, MO: Gospel Publishing House, 1968.

Duewel, Wesley. *Touch the World Through Prayer.* Grand Rapids, MI: Zondervan Publishing House, 1986.

Evans, W. I. *This River Must Flow.* Springfield, MO: Gospel Publishing House, 1954.

Fitzpatrick, Graham. *Miracles, Faith, and God's Will.* NSW, Australia: Spiritual Growth Publications, 1987.

Gramenz, Stuart, *How You Can Heal the Sick.* Chichester, ENG: Sovereign World. 1986.

Horton, Stanley M. *Pneumatology.* Brussels: International Correspondence Institute, 1979.

_____. *What the Bible Says About the Holy Spirit.* Springfield, MO: Gospel Publishing House, 1976.

Jeter, Hugh. *By His Stripes.* Springfield, MO: Gospel Publishing House, 1977.

Bibliography

Ladd, George Eldon. "The Gospel of the Kingdom," in *Perspectives on the World Christian Movement, A Reader.* Pasadena, CA: William Carey Library, 1981.

Marshall, Tom. *Foundations for a Healing Ministry.* Chichester, West Sussex: Sovereign World, 1988.

Miller, Jim B. Unpublished monograph "How to Heal the Sick."

Osborn, T. L. *How to Receive Miracle Healing.* Nairobi: Evangel Publishing House, 1955.

Pyches, David, *Spiritual Gifts in the Local Church.* Minneapolis: Bethany House Publishers, 1985.

Reddin, Opal, ed. *Power Encounter, A Pentecostal Perspective.* Springfield, MO: Central Bible College, 1989.

Stamps, Don C., ed. *The Full Life Study Bible, KJV.* Grand Rapids: Zondervan, 1992.

Sumerall, Lester. *Demons, the Answer Book.* South Bend, IN: LeSEA Publishing Co., 1979.

Williams, Don. *Signs, Wonders, and the Kingdom of God.* Ann Arbor, MI: Servant Publications, 1989.

Wimber, John, with Springer, Kevin. *Power Evangelism.* San Francisco: Harper and Row Publishers, 1986.

Wimber John. *Power Healing.* San Francisco: Harper and Row Publishers, 1987.

York, John. *Missions in the Age of the Spirit.* Springfield, MO: Logion Press, 2000.

– OTHER BOOKS BY DENZIL R. MILLER –

Power Ministry: How to Minister in the Spirit's Power (2004)
(also available in French, Portuguese, Malagasy,
Swahili, Kinyarwanda, and Chichewa)

*Empowered for Global Mission: A Missionary Look at
the Book of Acts* (2005)

From Azusa to Africa to the Nations (2005)
(also available in French, Spanish, and Portuguese)

Acts: The Spirit of God in Mission (2007)

In Step with the Spirit: Studies in the Spirit-filled Walk (2008)

*The Kingdom and the Power: The Kingdom of God:
A Pentecostal Interpretation* (2009)

*Experiencing the Spirit: A Study of the Work of the Spirit
in the Life of the Believer* (2009)

Teaching in the Spirit (2009)

*Power Encounter: Ministering in the Power and
Anointing of the Holy Spirit: Revised* (2009)
(also available in Kiswahili)

*You Can Minister in God's Power: A Guide for
Spirit-filled Disciples* (2009)
*The Spirit of God in Mission: A Vocational Commentary
on the Book of Acts* (2011)

*Proclaiming Pentecost: 100 Sermon Outlines on
he Power of the Holy Spirit* (2011) (Associate editor with Mark
Turney, editor) (Available in French, Spanish,
Portuguese, and Swahili)

Globalizing Pentecostal Missions in Africa (2011)
Editor, with Enson Lwesya)

The 1:8 Promise of Jesus: The Key to World Harvest (2012)

_____

All books are available on the Internet or by emailing
the author at denny.miller@agmd.org

_____

©2013 Denzil R. Miller
Published by PneumaLife Publications
3766 N Delaware Ave.
Springfield, MO, USA, 65803
Springfield, MO, U S A
Printed in the United States of America

www.ingramcontent.com/pod-product-compliance
Lightning Source LLC
Chambersburg PA
CBHW061652040426
42446CB00010B/1699